Introduction

We gain great insight when we read and study the Bible. Often we draw p... lives of Biblical characters whose personalities, circumstances, and challenges are surprisingly similar to our own. Their examples speak positively into our present-day lives.

Utilizing the DISC Personality System, this profile helps you not only identify your Personality Style, but also discover which Biblical characters are most similar to you. Biblical passages for Biblical characters are also suggested for further study.

The Biblical Profile has practical applications in everyday life. See how people are motivated in distinct ways, learn to minimize misunderstand-ings and appreciate the differences in others. Use this information to understand and appreciate your strengths and limitations so that you can grow in your relationship with God and others.

Contents

Introduction	1
Understanding Personality Styles	2
Personality System Profile	3
Scoring	4-5
Graph Description	6
What DISC Measures and Overview of Styles	7-9
Enhancing Communication	10
Pattern Descriptions with Biblical Character Match	11-36
Special DISC Patterns	37

© Copyright 2000-2020 by The Institute for Motivational Living, Inc. All Rights Reserved.

Understanding Personality Styles

Personality Styles are the language of **observable behavior**. Our primary style can tell us a great deal about how we are motivated, environments we prefer, our greatest fears, how we communicate and how we like others to communicate with us.

In the course of your daily routine, you see a variety of personality styles. As you observe fellow workers, friends, and family members, you'll see different personalities unfold right before your eyes. **Think about the people you know...**

- Do you know someone who is assertive, to the point and wants the bottom line? Some people are forceful, direct, and strong-willed. **They are examples of the D Style**.

  D = Drive • Challenge

- Do you have any friends who are great communicators and friendly to everyone they meet? Some people are optimistic, friendly and talkative. **They are examples of the I Style**.

  I = Influencing • Relationships

- Do you have any family members who are good listeners and great team players? Some people are steady, patient, loyal and practical. **They are examples of the S Style**.

  S = Steadiness • Consistency

- Have you ever worked with someone who enjoys gathering facts and details and is thorough in all activities? Some people are precise, sensitive and analytical. **They are examples of the C Style**.

  C = Compliance • Constraints

Instructions for completing the assessment:

1. Choose the setting or environment in which your responses will be made. (i.e. at work, at home, at church, in ministry, etc.)
2. Each box contains four phrases. Carefully read each of the four phrases in each box.
3. Keeping in mind the setting or environment you selected in step 1:
   Circle the ◆ next to the phrase that is MOST like you
   Circle the ● next to the phrase that is LEAST like you

   NOTE: - For each box, choose only ONE MOST and ONE LEAST response
   - Page 3 is carbon paper. Use a pen and press firmly for best results.
   - Your answers will be transfered to the page beneath (page 5).
4. This assessment should be completed in seven minutes (or as close to that as possible).
5. Once you have answered all of the questions, go to Page 5.

DISCinsights® Personality System Questionnaire

← Circle your answers on this page (3)
Answers appear on the next page (5) →

EXAMPLE 1:

M	L	
◆	●	Easy-going, Agreeable
◆	⦿	Trusting, Believing in others
◆	●	Adventurous, Risk taker
⬥	●	Tolerant, Respectful

EXAMPLE 2 (SIDE):

M	L	
S	S	Easy-going, Agreeable
I	Ⓘ	Trusting, Believing in others
★	D	Adventurous, Risk taker
Ⓒ	C	Tolerant, Respectful

Column 1

M	L	
◆	●	Easy-going, Agreeable
◆	●	Trusting, Believing in others
◆	●	Adventurous, Risk taker
◆	●	Tolerant, Respectful
◆	●	Soft spoken, Reserved
◆	●	Optimistic, Visionary
◆	●	Center of attention, Sociable
◆	●	Peacemaker, Bring harmony
◆	●	Encourage others
◆	●	Strive for perfection
◆	●	Be part of the team
◆	●	Want to establish goals
◆	●	Become frustrated
◆	●	Keep my feelings inside
◆	●	Tell my side of the story
◆	●	Stand up to opposition
◆	●	Lively, Talkative
◆	●	Fast paced, Determined
◆	●	Try to maintain balance
◆	●	Try to follow the rules
◆	●	Manage time efficiently
◆	●	Often rushed, Feel pressured
◆	●	Social things are important
◆	●	Like to finish what I start
◆	●	Resist sudden change
◆	●	Tend to over promise
◆	●	Withdraw under pressure
◆	●	Not afraid to fight
◆	●	A good encourager
◆	●	A good listener
◆	●	A good analyzer
◆	●	A good delegator

Column 2

M	L	
◆	●	Results are what matter
◆	●	Do it right, Accuracy counts
◆	●	Make it enjoyable
◆	●	Let's do it together
◆	●	Will do without, Self-controlled
◆	●	Will buy on impulse
◆	●	Will wait, No pressure
◆	●	Will spend on what I want
◆	●	Friendly, Easy to be with
◆	●	Unique, Bored by routine
◆	●	Actively change things
◆	●	Want things exact
◆	●	Non-confrontational, Giving in
◆	●	Overloaded with details
◆	●	Changes at the last minute
◆	●	Demanding, Abrupt
◆	●	Want advancement
◆	●	Satisfied with things, Content
◆	●	Openly display feelings
◆	●	Humble, Modest
◆	●	Cool, Reserved
◆	●	Happy, Carefree
◆	●	Pleasing, Kind
◆	●	Bold, Daring
◆	●	Spend quality time with others
◆	●	Plan for the future, Be prepared
◆	●	Travel to new adventures
◆	●	Receive rewards for goals met
◆	●	Rules need to be challenged
◆	●	Rules make it fair
◆	●	Rules make it boring
◆	●	Rules make it safe

Column 3

M	L	
◆	●	Education, Culture
◆	●	Achievements, Awards
◆	●	Safety, Security
◆	●	Social, Group Gatherings
◆	●	Take charge, Direct approach
◆	●	Outgoing, Enthusiastic
◆	●	Predictable, Consistent
◆	●	Cautious, Careful
◆	●	Not easily defeated
◆	●	Will do as told, Follows leader
◆	●	Excitable, Cheerful
◆	●	Want things orderly, Neat
◆	●	I will lead them
◆	●	I will follow through
◆	●	I will persuade them
◆	●	I will get the facts
◆	●	Think of others first
◆	●	Competitive, Like a challenge
◆	●	Optimistic, Positive
◆	●	Logical thinker, Systematic
◆	●	Please others, Agreeable
◆	●	Laugh out loud, Animated
◆	●	Courageous, Bold
◆	●	Quiet, Reserved
◆	●	Want more authority
◆	●	Want new opportunities
◆	●	Avoid any conflict
◆	●	Want clear directions
◆	●	Reliable, Dependable
◆	●	Creative, Unique
◆	●	Bottom line, Results oriented
◆	●	Hold high standards, Accurate

© Copyright 2000-2020 by The Institute for Motivational Living, Inc. All Rights Reserved.

DISCinsights® Personality System Graph Page

Scoring Instructions:
1. **Row 1:** Total the "D" values from **all three** "M" columns on pg. 5. Enter the totals in the "Most-D" block below. Repeat the process for the "I," "S," "C" and "★" totals. Total of all blocks in Row 1 must equal 24.
2. **Row 2:** Total the "D" values from **all three** "L" columns on pg. 5. Enter the totals in the "Least-D" block below. Repeat the process for the "I," "S," "C" and "★" totals. Total of all blocks in Row 2 must equal 24.
3. **Row 3:** Subtract Row 2 from Row 1. Enter the totals in the "Change-D" block below. Repeat the process for the "I," "S," and "C" scores. Do not calculate the "★" score. *(Example: If your MOST D score is 4 and the LEAST score is 8 then your CHANGE score = -4)*

		D	I	S	C	★	Total Score
Row 1	First, enter the "MOST" scores in Row 1 →	**Most**					Must Equal **24**
Row 2	Next, enter the "LEAST" scores in Row 2 →	**Least**					Must Equal **24**
Row 3	Then, subtract Row 2 from Row 1 →	**Change**					Do not calculate ★ value for Row 3

NOTE: If the Row 2 ("LEAST") number is larger than the Row 1 ("MOST") number, the number will be negative ("-") in Row 3.
REMEMBER: The "+" and "-" numbers can ONLY be plotted on GRAPH 3.

Graphing Instructions:
1. **Graph 1:** Use the numbers for D, I, S, C from the MOST row to plot Graph 1 by placing a dot on (or near) the number on the graphs.
2. **Graph 2:** Use the numbers for D, I, S, C from the LEAST row to plot Graph 2 by placing a dot on (or near) the number on the graphs.
3. **Graph 3:** Use the numbers from the CHANGE row to plot Graph 3. Pay attention to positive and negative numbers.
4. Draw a straight line to connect the D - I - S - C dots on each of the three graphs. See example below.

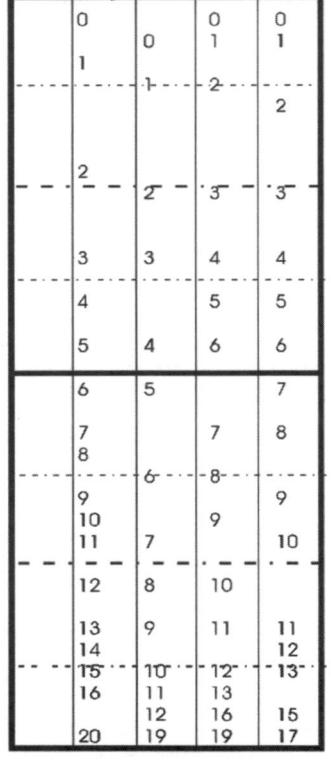

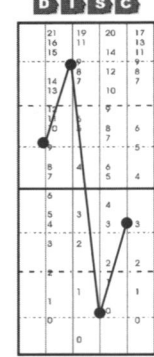

Example:

Note: If you cannot find the exact number for your score on a graph, estimate between the two closest numbers on any given line.

© Copyright 2000-2020 by The Institute for Motivational Living, Inc. All Rights Reserved.

DISCinsights® Personality System Tally Sheet

Adding Instructions:
1. Count the number of times you circled "D" in **all three** "M" columns below. Write that number in the MOST row under the "D" on page 4. Repeat the process for the "I," "S," "C," and "★" scores.
2. Count the number of times you circled "D" in **all three** "L" columns below. Write that number in the LEAST row under the "D" on page 4. Repeat the process for the "I," "S," "C," and "★" scores.

M	L		M	L		M	L	
S	S		D	D		★	C	
I	I		C	C		D	D	
★	D		★	I		S	S	
C	C		★	S		I	★	
C	★		★	C		D	D	
D	D		D	D		★	I	
★	I		S	S		★	S	
S	S		I	★		C	★	
I	I		S	★		D	D	
★	C		★	I		S	★	
★	S		D	D		I	I	
D	★		C	C		★	C	
C	C		★	S		D	★	
S	S		C	★		S	S	
★	I		I	I		I	I	
D	D		D	D		C	★	
I	★		D	D		S	S	
D	D		S	★		D	D	
S	S		I	★		I	I	
★	C		★	C		★	C	
C	★		C	C		S	S	
D	D		I	I		★	I	
I	I		S	★		D	D	
S	S		D	D		C	C	
S	★		S	S		★	D	
I	I		C	★		I	★	
★	C		I	I		S	S	
★	D		D	D		★	C	
I	I		★	D		★	S	
S	S		C	★		I	I	
C	C		I	I		D	★	
D	D		S	S		C	★	

© Copyright 2000-2020 by The Institute for Motivational Living, Inc. All Rights Reserved.

Graph Description

Graph 1
Mask, Public Self
Behavior Expected by Others

Everyone acts according to how they think other people expect them to act.

This behavior is the public self, the person projected to others.

Sometimes, there is no difference between the true person and their public self. However, the public self can be very different from the "real" person: it is often called "a Mask" or the person we think others "expect" to see.

Graph 1 is generated by the "Most" choices on The Personality System, and has the greatest potential for change.

Graph 2
Core, Private Self
Instinctive Response to Pressure

Everyone has learned responses from the past; consequently, these are behaviors which the person accepts about him/herself. Under pressure or tension, these learned behaviors become prominent.

This is the graph which is the least likely to change because these are natural and ingrained responses. A person's behavior under pressure may be drastically different than his/her behavior in Graphs 1 and 3.

Graph 3
Mirror, Perceived Self
Self-Image, Self-Identity

Everyone envisions him/her self in a particular way. Graph 3 displays the mental picture that one has of him/her self, the self image or self identity.

Graph 3 combines the learned responses from one's past with the current expected behavior from the environment.

Change in one's perception can occur, but it is usually gradual and based on the changing demands of one's environment.

Different Graphs Indicate Change or Transition

If Graph 1 is different than Graph 2, the demands of the environment are forcing behavior that is not congruent with the core, or instinctive behavior. In such a situation, a person trying to modify his/her behavior to meet the demands of the environment will most likely experience stress.

If Graph 1 is different than Graph 2, but similar to Graph 3, the individual has been able to successfully alter his/her behavior to meet the demands of the environment without altering his/her core. This individual is probably fairly comfortable with the behavior shown in Graph 3 (Perceived Self), and is probably not experiencing stress.

If Graph 1 is different than Graph 3, an individual may be in a period of growth (and some discomfort) while he/she attempts to alter behavior to meet the demands of a new environment. A person's behavior may fluctuate during this period of adjustment.

Similar Graphs Indicate Few Demands For Change

An individual who perceives the current demands of the environment (Graph 1) to be similar to his/her past (Graph 2) will have little need to change his/her self-perception (Graph 3). This may be due to any of the following factors:

The behavior demanded by the present environment is similar to demands in the past.

This individual controls what others demand of him/her.

The behavior demanded by the present environment is different than demands in the past. However, instead of altering behavior, this person has chosen to augment style. To accomplish augmentation, this individual has surrounded him/herself with people of complimentary styles, thus creating a team with combined strengths.

What DISC Measures

 **MEASURES HOW A PERSON SOLVES PROBLEMS AND RESPONDS TO CHALLENGES...**

INTENSITY
The higher the D value, the more active and intense an individual will be in trying to overcome problems and obstacles. The lower the D value, the greater the tendency to gather data prior to making a decision.

WHEN IN AN ANTAGONISTIC ENVIRONMENT
The high D responds aggressively and directly.

EMOTION
The D factor measures the emotion of anger. Extremely high Ds are quick to anger. Extremely low Ds are slow to anger.

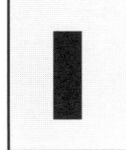 **MEASURES HOW A PERSON ATTEMPTS TO INFLUENCE OR PERSUADE OTHERS...**

INTENSITY
The higher the I value, the more verbal and persuasive the person will be in trying to influence others to his/her way of thinking. The lower the I value, the more the person will use data and facts.

WHEN IN AN ANTAGONISTIC ENVIRONMENT
The high I responds actively and may try to negotiate an agreement or apologize quickly.

EMOTION
The I factor measures the emotion of optimism. Extremely high Is are joyful and optimistic. Low Is tend to be more pessimistic.

 **MEASURES HOW A PERSON RESPONDS TO THE RULES AND REGULATIONS SET BY OTHERS...**

INTENSITY
The higher the C value, the more the person will comply to rules set by others. The lower the C value, the more an individual will challenge rules and seek independence.

WHEN IN AN ANTAGONISTIC ENVIRONMENT
High C's will respond passively/aggressively and seek to justify their actions.

EMOTION
The C factor measures caution. The higher the intensity of the C, the more an individual cautiously and analytically moves forward. The lower the C value, the more fearless the individual.

 **MEASURES THE PACE AT WHICH A PERSON RESPONDS TO CHANGE...**

INTENSITY
The higher the S value, the more the person prefers to start and complete one project at a time. Also, the higher the S, the more resistant to change. The lower the S value, the faster the pace and greater is the desire for change.

WHEN IN AN ANTAGONISTIC ENVIRONMENT
The high S will respond passively and seek to blend in to situations.

EMOTION
The S factor measures emotional expression. The higher the S value, the more difficult it is to read an individual. The lower the S factor, the more a person is expressive of their emotions.

The Personality System Overview

ACTIVE STYLES

TASK-ORIENTED STYLES

DOMINANT • DRIVER
Determined

Likes to Take on Active Roles and is Task Oriented

General Characteristics: Good problem solver, risk taker, strong ego, self-starter, goal-oriented

Value To Team: Bottom-line organizer
Places high value on time
Challenges the status quo
Innovative
Motivator

Challenge Areas: Oversteps authority
Argumentative attitude
Dislikes routine
Attempts too much at once

Greatest Fear: Being taken advantage of

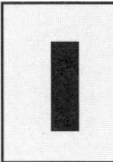

INFLUENCING • INSPIRING
Impulsive

Likes to Take on Active Roles and is People Oriented

General Characteristics: Enthusiastic, trusting, optimistic, persuasive, talkative, impulsive, emotional

Value To Team: Creative problem-solver
Great encourager
Motivates others to achieve
Positive sense of humor
Negotiates conflicts; peace-maker

Challenge Areas: Inattentive to detail
More concerned with popularity than tangible results
Overuses gestures and facial expressions
Tends to listen only when it's convenient

Greatest Fear: Rejection

COMPLIANT • CORRECT
Cautious

Likes to Take on Passive Roles and is Task Oriented

General Characteristics: Accurate, analytical, conscientious, careful, fact-finder, precise, high standards, systematic

Value To Team: Perspective: "The anchor of reality"
Conscientious and even-tempered,
Thorough in all activities
Defines situations
Gathers, criticizes and tests information

Challenge Areas: Gets bogged down in details
Needs clear-cut boundaries for actions/relationships
Bound by procedures and methods
Prefers not to verbalize feelings
Sensitive to criticism

Greatest Fear: Criticism

STABLE • STEADY
Supportive

Likes to Take on Passive Roles and is People Oriented

General Characteristics: Good listener, team player, possessive, steady, predictable, understanding, friendly

Value To Team: Reliable and dependable
Loyal team worker
Compliant towards authority
Good listener; patient and empathetic
Good at reconciling conflicts

Challenge Areas: Resists change
Takes a long time to adjust to change
Holds a grudge
Will give in rather than argue
Difficulty establishing priorities

Greatest Fear: Loss of security

PASSIVE STYLES

Highlighting Your Individual Style

Instructions:
Step 1: Identify your highest plotting point on Graph 3. If Graph 2 is drastically different, look at it also.
Step 2: Refer to the quadrant below that corresponds with that highest point (D, I, S, or C)
Step 3: Mark "+" if the word or statement describes you.
Mark "o" if the word or statement does not describe you.
Step 4: Identify your second highest plotting point on the graph, refer to that quadrant below and repeat step 3.

D

My personal behavior is...
- __Demanding
- __Determined
- __Driving
- __Ambitious
- __Pioneering
- __Strong-willed
- __Competitive
- __Decisive
- __Responsible
- __Skeptical
- __Logical
- __Independent

I am motivated by...
- __New challenges and problems to solve
- __Power and authority to take risks and make decisions
- __Freedom from routine and mundane tasks
- __Changing environments in which to work and play

My ideal environment should include...
- __Innovative focus on the future
- __Non-routine, challenging tasks & activities
- __Projects that produce tangible results
- __Freedom from controls, supervision and details
- __Personal evaluation based on my results, not my methods

I

My personal behavior is...
- __Sociable
- __Optimistic
- __Mobile
- __Polished
- __Enthusiastic
- __Persuasive
- __Warm
- __Poised
- __Trusting
- __Popular
- __Verbal
- __Independent

I am motivated by...
- __Flattery, praise, popularity, and acceptance
- __A friendly environment
- __Freedom from many rules and regulations
- __Other people available to handle details

My ideal environment should include...
- __Practical procedures
- __Few conflicts and arguments
- __Freedom from controls and details
- __A forum to express ideas

C

My personal behavior is...
- __Conservative
- __Calculating
- __Low-keyed
- __Stable
- __Dependent
- __Cautious
- __Traditional
- __Neat
- __Systematic
- __Accurate
- __Tactful
- __Diplomatic

I am motivated by...
- __Standards of high quality
- __Limited social interaction
- __Detailed tasks
- __Logical organization of information

My ideal environment should include...
- __Tasks and projects that can be followed through to completion
- __Specialized or technical tasks
- __Practical work procedures and routines
- __Few conflicts and arguments
- __Instructions and reassurance that I am doing what is expected of me

S

My personal behavior is...
- __Conservative
- __Loyal
- __Cooperative
- __Relaxed
- __Resistant to change
- __Reflective
- __Systematic
- __Passive
- __Patient
- __Possessive
- __Predictable
- __Consistent
- __Steady
- __Deliberate

I am motivated by...
- __Recognition for loyalty and dependability
- __Safety and security
- __No sudden changes in procedure or lifestyle
- __Activities I can start and finish

My ideal environment should include...
- __Practical procedures and systems
- __Stability and predictability
- __Tasks that can be completed one at a time
- __Few conflicts and arguments
- __A team atmosphere

Enhancing Communication

The primary "D" loves it when you...

- Are brief, direct, and to-the-point when explaining yourself
- Ask "what" not "how" questions
- Focus on the results (remember they desire results)
- Give them the "bottom line" when describing a situation
- Suggest ways to help them solve problems
- Highlight the benefits when telling them about your ideas
- Agree with facts rather than emotions when agreeing with them
- Discuss a problem in light of how it will slow results

But has difficulty understanding when you...

- Ramble or repeat yourself
- Focus on problems instead of solutions
- Make generalizations
- Make statements without support

The primary "I" loves it when you...

- Give them an opportunity to talk about their ideas, other people, and their emotions
- Assist them in developing ways to transfer talk into action
- Share your ideas and experiences with them
- Recognize them for their accomplishments
- Give them the opportunity to motivate & influence others
- Show them that you accept them
- Explain the details, but don't dwell on them
- Communicate with them in a friendly & light manner

But has difficulty understanding when you...

- Do all the talking
- Eliminate their social time
- Ignore their ideas and accomplishments
- Tell them what to do without asking their input
- Give them the "detail" work

The primary "C" loves it when you...

- Support your ideas with accurate information
- Are specific when explaining yourself
- Are patient, persistent, and diplomatic while providing explanations
- Agree with facts rather than emotions when agreeing with them
- Allow them their space and independence
- Tell them up front your expectations of them
- Give them the pros and cons of an argument

But has difficulty understanding when you...

- Refuse to explain the details
- Answer questions vaguely or casually
- Surprise them with new information

The primary "S" loves it when you...

- Express a genuine interest in them as a person
- Give them answers to "how" questions
- Clearly define your goals, a procedure, or their role in the overall plan
- Are patient with them
- Give them your sincere appreciation
- Give them time to adjust to changes
- Present ideas or changes in a nonthreatening manner
- Provide them with feedback

But has difficulty understanding when you...

- Are pushy or overly aggressive
- Are demanding
- Are confrontational

Pattern Description

Instructions:

Step 1: Using Graph 3 of your profile, look at all of your plotting points that are above the midline. Determine your primary characteristic (highest point) _AND_ your secondary characteristic (second highest point.)

Step 2: Refer to the quadrant below that corresponds to your HIGHEST plotting point (D, I, S, or C)

Step 3: Remaining in that quadrant, locate the combination of letters that depicts your highest and second highest point in order. For example: if your highest point is "D" and your second highest point is "I", this would be D • I - Concluder.

Step 4: If necessary, identify your THIRD highest point on your graph (must be above the midline) and locate the combination of letters which it matches. Example: "D", "I" and "S" equals D • I • S - Director.

Step 5: Turn to the page listed for your pattern name.

Behavior Style	Pattern Name	Turn to Page
Pure D	Establisher	23
D equal I	Influencer	25
D • C	Challenger	16
D • C • I	Chancellor	17
D • C • S	Attainer	15
D • I	Concluder	19
D • I • C	Chancellor	17
D • I • S	Director	22
D • S	Attainer	15
D • S • I	Director	22
D • S • C	Attainer	15

Behavior Style	Pattern Name	Turn to Page
Pure I	Communicator	18
I • C	Assessor	14
I • C • S	Governor	24
I • C • D	Leader	27
I • D	Persuader	32
I • D • C	Leader	27
I • D • S	Reformer	35
I • S	Advisor	12
I • S • C	Governor	24
I • S • D	Motivator	30

Behavior Style	Pattern Name	Turn to Page
Pure C	Logical Thinker	28
C • D	Designer	21
C • D • I	Chancellor	17
C • D • S	Contemplator	20
C • I	Assessor	14
C • I • D	Chancellor	17
C • I • S	Mediator	29
C • S	Precisionist	34
C • S • D	Contemplator	20
C • S • I	Practitioner	33

Behavior Style	Pattern Name	Turn to Page
Pure S	Technician	36
S • C	Peacemaker	31
S • C • D	Inquirer	26
S • C • I	Advocate	13
S • D	Attainer	15
S • D • C	Inquirer	26
S • D • I	Attainer	15
S • I	Advisor	12
S • I • C	Advocate	13
S • I • D	Attainer	15

© Copyright 2000-2020 by The Institute for Motivational Living, Inc. All Rights Reserved.

Advisor/Counselor/One Who Is Merciful

Advisor

Individuals who are **Advisors** exhibit warmth, sympathy and understanding in their approach to people. They possess a casual kind of poise in most social situations. Many people will come to them because Advisors are seen as good listeners. They typically do not attempt to force their ideas on others, and in a conflict are likely to yield or be overly flexible. If the conflict is serious, they may withdraw to avoid further conflict rather than work at resolution. They tend to take criticism of their work as a personal affront. They can sometimes be overly tolerant and patient with non producers. Advisors prefer to deal with people on a personal, intimate basis in a low-pressure situation. Their managers should realize that Advisors tend to allow too much lead time on projects. They need personal attention and compliments for assignments that are well done. Their best work will be done when a public viewing or review is likely. They are instinctive team players and work best in an environment of acceptance and serenity.

Advisors in Scripture	Scripture Verses To Study
Barnabas	Acts 4, 9, 11-15
Mary Magdalene	Luke 7:36-47; John 20:1-18
Elisha	1 Kings 19; 2 Kings 2-13
Nicodemus	John 3,7,19

Barnabas: Luke tells us that Barnabas was a name given to a Cypriot Levite named Joseph because he was a "Son of Encouragement" (Acts 4:36). Barnabas was drawn to people he could encourage and counsel. The apostle Paul must have known of his reputation, probably approaching him privately with news of his conversion and seeking a Christian friend. It would be Barnabas' nature to advise and encourage him; perhaps even discipling the newly converted Pharisee. It was Barnabas who brought Paul to the apostles in Jerusalem and built the relationship, overcoming their fears (Acts 9:26-7). When he and Paul disagreed about John Mark, Barnabas withdrew and chose to break off their relationship rather than working at a resolution (Acts 15:36-39). They went separate ways, Barnabas with Mark and Paul with Silas. Mark's eventual effective ministry, writing the Gospel of Mark, confirmed Barnabas' patient counsel and advice.

Mary Magdalene: Some believe that Mary Magdalene's desire to be accepted created moral difficulties in her lifestyle until she met someone who accepted her unconditionally, although the Scriptures do not definitively state that she was a prostitute. The pure love of Jesus transformed any other desires she may have had into absolute devotion. Her need for acceptance brought her to the home of Simon the Pharisee with her alabaster jar of perfume. She poured out herself and her gift in full sight of all, unconcerned with Simon's scorn. It was her loyalty that brought her to the foot of the cross, when fear stopped all but one of His apostles from being there.

Elisha: Elisha focused more on people than his mentor, Elijah, thus revealing his orientation toward people as he cared for widows and warned kings. His strong relational character was revealed in his devoted service to Elijah. He was willing to serve so he could gain power to do all to which God had called him.

Nicodemus: His desire to avoid conflict with the Sanhedrin caused him to first approach Jesus at night. The relationship they forged moved him to defend Jesus before them in John 7:51. We last see him at the garden tomb, embalming his friend and encouraging Joseph of Arimathea by his presence. (John 19:39)

Jesus as the Advisor: As the Advisor, people and relationships were clearly what Jesus valued most. *'Love the Lord your God with all your heart and with all your soul and with all your mind and with all your strength.' The second is this: 'Love your neighbor as yourself.' There is no commandment greater than these."* Mark 12:30,31

Graph Characteristics: The Advisor's graph is either I/S or S/I, characterized by having both the "I" and the "S" traits being exhibited above the midline, while both the "D" and the "C" traits remain below the midline. The relative position of the "I" and the "S" will determine if the individual is more active and communication focused (higher "I") or more passive and team focused (higher "S"). Both positions will be extremely people oriented.

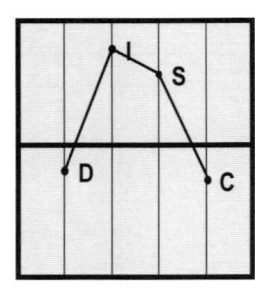

Advocate/Agent/One Who Makes Peace

Individuals who are **Advocates** are steady, sociable individuals who strive for positive relationships at work and at home. They can tend toward individualism and independence if "I" is their secondary characteristic. If "C" is their secondary characteristic, they will be more passive and detail oriented. Once they have made up their mind, it can be quite difficult to change the mind of an Advocate. They like people to support them and their ideas; they tend to support the underdog. They may take opposing sides of a disagreement and leave feeling frustrated if things don't go their way. Advocates need to be accepted as part of a team. Decisions can be difficult for them to make unless their boundaries are very clearly defined.

Advocates tend to be moderate, thorough, and dependable people. They are often willing to intercede for another on their behalf. They have a strong sense of justice and loyalty. This style is known for their common sense. They always try to think through both sides of an issue. Advocates also tend to be great peace makers, since they see many different viewpoints to an issue; and their peacemaking will focus on the people involved, not just the issue. Since Advocates are relational, they are very sensitive to the feelings of others.

Advocates in Scripture:	Scripture Verses To Study
Abraham	Genesis 17 through 24
John Mark	Acts 12:23-13:13, 15:36-39
Ruth	Ruth 2 and 3

Abraham: Abraham was a peacemaker. He told Sarah to do what she wished with her servant Hagar; he told Abimelech that Sarah was his sister. These decisions were driven by his desire to maintain peace in his environment. Abraham demonstrated the tendency of the Advocate to avoid aggression in his dealings with Lot in Genesis 13, "If you go to the left, I'll go to the right; if you go to the right, I'll go to the left." Abraham demonstrated the Advocate's loyalty in his desire to see his son Ishmael blessed in Gen 17:18. Abraham's ultimate test of loyalty was his willingness to sacrifice Isaac (Gen 22).

John Mark: Mark spent his early Christian life with Peter. He was likely the young man in the garden who ran away (Mark 14:51-52). Running continued to be an issue in Mark's life, rearing its head again with Barnabas and Paul. The Lord's maturing process and Barnabas' encouragement eventually developed this into a solid commitment. Mark challenges us to learn from our mistakes, and teaches us that we can overcome our past. Paul's final assessment of him – "He is helpful to me in my ministry". (2 Tim 4:11)

Ruth: Demonstrating her loyalty and the Advocate's tendency to support the underdog, Ruth accompanies her mother-in-law back to Bethlehem. The Advocate's determination when their mind is made up can be seen in her reply to Naomi - "Where you go I will go, and where you stay I will stay." (Ruth 1:16-17) Her loyalty became the means by which the Lord blessed her and met all her needs.

Jesus as the Advocate: Jesus clearly knew His role of authority because it was plainly put forth by the Father. An S/C/I or S/I/C can be a very effective leader with clear lines of authority. *By myself I can do nothing; I judge only as I hear, and my judgment is just, for I seek not to please myself but him who sent me. John 5:30*

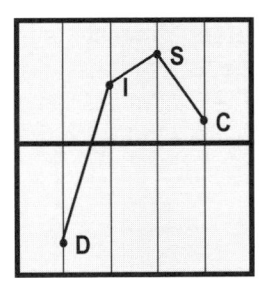

Graph Characteristics: The Advocate's graph is either S/C/I or S/I/C, characterized by having the "I", the "S" and the "C" traits being exhibited above the midline, while only the "D" trait remains below the midline. The relative position of the "I" and the "C" will determine if the individual will face inner conflicts over being both expressive and reserved. In any combination, the I/S/C blend can behave with the decisiveness and determination of a "D" if their parameters are clearly identified.

© Copyright 2000-2020 by The Institute for Motivational Living, Inc. All Rights Reserved.

Assessor/Reviewer/One Who Reveals Value

Assessor

Individuals who are **Assessors** are observant of details as well as the unique value of people. They combine a concern for particulars with an awareness and appreciation for the people needed to accomplish tasks; this lends to the development of open channels of communication. They will frequently express an enthusiasm and optimism for accomplishing tasks, as well as being an encouraging influence to those around them. These are traits they derive from the "I" influence of the character. However, their enthusiasm will be based upon a thorough assessment of the factors required to achieve the goal, and their encouragement will be directed to the accomplishment of the task at hand. Assessors are typically excellent judges of character, and will easily trust those who meet their standards.

Assessors can be counted on to do a good job, to value their associates and to pay attention to details. They have a tendency to be competitive with themselves; they push themselves to do better in order to avoid any rejection or criticism. People who have this style often have a unique teaching gift.

Assessors in Scripture:	**Scripture Verses To Study**
Miriam	Exodus 15-21; Numbers 12:1-15
Ezra	Ezra 7,8
Shunammite Woman	2 Kings 4: 8-37

Miriam: Moses' older sister, Miriam, was a prophetess and leader in the Israelites' exodus out of Egypt. A musician and poet like David, she lead the Israelite women in praising God after He caused the sea to close over the pursuing Egyptians. She was cheerful and optimistic and everyone followed her example. Miriam's passion to do things according to the law is seen in her protesting Moses' Cushite wife. Hebrews were not to intermarry, and this marriage was "against the rules" in Miriam's eyes. She preferred to avoid conflict, choosing to "discuss" the issue with Aaron instead of going directly to the root of the problem and sharing her feelings with Moses. Her desire for correctness won out over her inclination towards relationship, and God reprimanded her. By the time of her death, Miriam had become such a social figure that her passing was considered a great loss to the community and a shortened version of her name, Mary, was given to many women to commemorate her legacy.

Ezra: Ezra was a man who was devoted to his studies. His natural orientation shines as he organizes family groups heading to Jerusalem, while the people side of Ezra allowed him to lead and inspire hundreds of people on such a journey. As a leader, a priest and a scribe, we see not only his attention to details but also his ability to influence others to be so committed.

Shunammite Woman: This woman took delight in offering hospitality, and she was a frequent hostess to Elisha. Her desire to be pleasing to a "Man of God" is so strong that she convinces her husband to build Elisha his own room. Her questioning tendencies come to light as she wants to trust Elisha's news of motherhood for her, but asks for reassurance. When her son dies, she designs and executes her plan as quickly as possible as she seeks Elisha's aid in restoring him back to life.

Jesus as the Assessor: Jesus was a great communicator in front of a large crowd, all the while remembering how important every detail of prophecy was. *In the same way, let your light shine before men, that they may see your good deeds and praise your Father in heaven. Do not think that I have come to abolish the Law or the Prophets; I have not come to abolish them but to fulfill them. I tell you the truth, until heaven and earth disappear, not the smallest letter, not the least stroke of a pen, will by any means disappear from the Law until everything is accomplished. Matthew 5:16-18*

Graph Characteristics: The Assessor's graph is either I/C or C/I, characterized by having both the "I" and the "C" traits being exhibited above the midline, while both the "D" and the "S" traits remain below the midline. The relative position of the "I" and the "C" will determine if the individual is more verbally focused (higher "I") or more detail focused (higher "C").

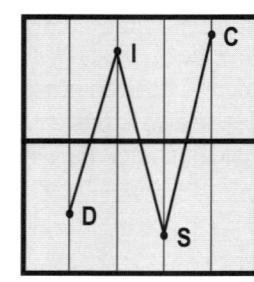

Attainer/Achiever/One Who Perseveres

Individuals who are **Attainers** exhibit an objective and analytical style. They can be fiercely independent, but also enjoy working well as part of a team. Attainers derive their motivation from internal rather than external sources; typically from personal goals and an inner drive to complete a task and be considered "righteous" or "a winner." Their task focus may override consideration for others, causing them to appear uncaring and distant. When relationships are not good, this will cause them some internal turmoil. They display a dogged determination, and can be successful at many things. Their calm and steady character makes them a good leader, and gives them the ability to "plan their work and work their plan". Their resolute disposition contributes to their success, even when faced with significant obstacles. Attainers may focus more on achieving the goal than on who achieves the goal with them. Because this style does not quit easily and has the ability to "hang in there" for long periods of time, they need to be encouraged to value and work on relationships, not simply the tasks involved in reaching a goal.

Attainers in Scripture:	Scripture Verses To Study
Daniel	Daniel 1-6
Job	Job 1:5, James 5:11
Martha (Lazarus' Sister)	Luke 10:38-42

Daniel: Daniel displayed the inner drive of the Attainer and it kept him loyal to his God. Even as a teenager in the courts of Babylon he "resolved not to defile himself" (Daniel 1:8). His determination and leadership had a profound effect on Shadrach, Meshach and Abednego, probably laying the groundwork for their later willingness to remain undefiled, despite the king's command (Daniel 3:16-18). Daniel's fierce independence and inner drive to be righteous is evident in his refusal to stop praying three times a day to the Lord, even when he knew it could very well cost him his life. (Daniel 6:10). Even his enemies "could find no corruption in him" when they were intent on destroying him, "because he was trustworthy and neither corrupt nor negligent" (Daniel 6:4). Daniel challenges Attainers to stand up for what is right, and to determine to use their commitment to high standards as a positive influence on those around them.

Job: Job offered a daily sacrifice for each of his children in case they had committed some sin. In this he showed both his perseverance and his desire to be considered "righteous". His commitment to high standards caused him to stubbornly hold on to his conviction that Yahweh was good. Neither Satan's attack nor his wife's pressure ("Are you still holding on to your integrity? Curse God and die!") could sway him (Job 2:9). Though his "comforters" accuse every aspect of his character Job perseveres. Displaying the characteristics of the Attainer, he became stubborn and distant, finally even displaying his annoyance and answering them with sarcasm and ridicule in Job 26-31.

Martha: Martha displayed the Attainers irritation and distance in the manner in which she confronted her sister's lack of assistance - right in front of all the other guests! She wasn't concerned about Mary's self esteem, only about her working on the task at hand. Her task focus was corrected by Jesus (Luke 10:41-2); relationships are important to the advancement of the Kingdom. The industrious nature of the Attainer shows in Martha opening her home to Jesus in Luke 10, and in her going out to meet Him though Lazarus lay dead (John 11:20). Even in grief, doing the right thing by greeting her guest was important to her. Attainers persevere in relationships, seeking high standards and loyalty in their friendships.

Jesus as the Attainer: A person of compassion, Jesus was not afraid of a confrontation to protect the security of someone in need. When the woman caught in adultery was brought to Him, Jesus very gently but firmly took control of the situation and confronted the woman's accusers. He then confronted the sin in the woman's life condemning only her actions. *John 8:1-11*

Graph Characteristics: The Attainer's graph is either D/S or S/D, characterized by having both the "D" and the "S" traits being exhibited above the midline, while both the "I" and the "C" traits remain below the midline. The relative position of the "D" and the "S" will determine if the individual is more task focused (higher "D") or more team focused (higher "S").

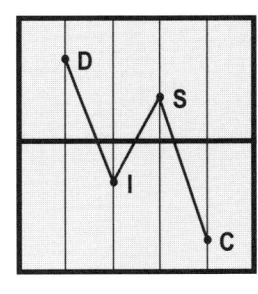

Challenger/Confronter/One Who Searches

Individuals who are **Challengers** exhibit an awareness of problems coupled with a creative character. Due to their strong resolve, they can complete significant tasks in very little time. Using a great deal of foresight, they examine all possible avenues when searching for a solution to a problem or focusing on a project. Equal striving for correctness counterbalances their drive for tangible results. They are perfectionistic and may vacillate in decision making. Challengers prefer working alone and resent restrictions. Searching for details and facts, especially about the unfamiliar, they sometimes ignore the emotional side of people. Their greatest fear is not being influential or of failing. They do not get personally involved, as they are very task oriented and driven mainly by results. Although they are emotionally restrained, a Challenger will speak the truth in any situation. They are willing and able to challenge the status quo when they perceive a better way. They are not typically afraid to confront even significant superiors with an issue. Challengers may be perceived as uncaring, since they focus on facts and outcomes more than feelings and relationships.

Challengers must learn to pace themselves and be cautious of working too much without time for relaxation. Since their standards are high, they have a tendency to be hard on themselves. They are excellent administrators and will find the way to get the job done.

Challengers in Scripture:	Scripture Verses To Study
Malachi	Malachi 4
Nathan	2 Samuel 12:1-13
Nahum	Nahum 1-3

Malachi: In a time of great unfaithfulness to God, Malachi was the voice that challenged the Israelites to return to their Lord. Malachi knew the rules very well. He knew when they were broken and he would not tolerate anything less than complete obedience to God. As a result, God used him to do whatever it took to accomplish His goal of exposing the unfaithfulness among His people. Malachi was so committed to fulfilling his calling the right way that he did not hesitate to pronounce the Lord's judgement to a sinful people.

Nathan: Nathan displayed a combination of creativity and direction as he confronted David about his rendezvous with Bathsheba. He knew how to get David's attention by opening with a striking story, and immediately pinned the guilt on David. A true Challenger, Nathan would not tolerate anything less than complete obedience to God. His direct "You are that man" demonstrates the fact that Challengers tend to focus on facts versus feelings.

Nahum: Nahum was used by God to prophesy against one of the most powerful nations of his time, Assyria. In the face of danger, Nahum spoke the truth of God to this empire. He was used to disclose details of the situation and articulate the complete truth of God without compromise -- and without regard for his or anyone else's feelings.

Jesus as the Challenger: Jesus challenged the Pharisees and reminded them of their shortcomings, because they were guilty of unfairly judging. While Jesus pardoned sinners, He pointed out the faults of those who should have been compassionate on the lost ones they were not shepherding. *Woe to you, teachers of the law and Pharisees, you hypocrites! You shut the kingdom of heaven in men's faces. You yourselves do not enter, nor will you let those enter who are trying to. Matthew 23:13*

Graph Characteristics: The Challenger's graph is D/C, characterized by having both the "D" and the "C" traits being exhibited above the midline, while both the "I" and the "S" traits remain below the midline. The "D" will be higher above the midline than the "C".

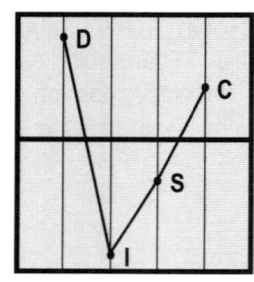

Chancellor/Judge/One Who Upholds Truth

Individuals who are **Chancellors** exhibit an energetic style trying to keep others focused in order to get things done. Outgoing by nature, they enjoy people; but this does not necessarily mean allegiance. They are determined individuals who are very sociable, but they also make sure the details are attended to. Chancellors want things to be done properly, and they may finish projects themselves to assure correctness and completeness as they desire respect and control. They sometimes neglect careful planning and may jump into projects without thorough consideration. However, they require precision and are very aware of the deadlines. A Chancellor will seldom hesitate to initiate activity. They are driven by the end results and desire to reach them quickly. They work tenaciously to resolve problems, combining accuracy with quick thinking. Under pressure, Chancellors tend to express their feelings without allowing others to share their opinions. When in dialogue, they want others to communicate clearly and concisely. Chancellors are always looking ahead to what new and exciting adventures they can jump into next.

Chancellors in Scripture:
Paul
Canaanite Woman
Jephthah

Scripture Verses To Study
Acts 9:1-29, 28:30
Matthew 15: 22-28
Judges 11

Paul: One of the best known New Testament writers, Paul was a Chancellor in his own time. His "do it now" task-orientation drove him on. Paul was constantly engaging in conversation or some sort of communication with others, usually concerning Christ. He was a very powerful communicator, and every message he delivered was sure to leave its mark. In Acts 9:2, driven to take action upon his beliefs, he obtains a letter consenting to persecution of Jesus' followers. His logical element is evident from his training as a Pharisee; he knows all 632 of the Mosaic laws, and as a Christian, he is able to logically dispute them.

Canaanite Woman: Jesus called her a woman of great faith (Matthew 15:28). Her need to find truth is immediately visible as she seeks him out, a very uncustomary practice in that day. She has no difficulty in communicating with him and convincing him to heal her daughter. Determined, she uses logic to prove her point - stating facts and not using emotional words. She was a Chancellor working to get the task done quickly and correctly. Notice her seeking justice - "Even the dogs eat the crumbs that fall from their Master's table."

Jepthah: Jepthath, who began his life as an outcast, seemed to attract people wherever he went. In Judges 11:3 we see "adventurers" gathered around him, even in a foreign land. Elders of his hometown recognized him as a strong leader, but their previous treachery causes him to require proof of their intentions. True to the Chancellor style, Jepthath sometimes forgot to look before he leaped. In verses 30-31, he made a promise without considering all the possible outcomes, and ended up having to sacrifice his daughter. His strong commitment to uphold his word won out in the end, he kept his promise and did exactly what he said he would.

Jesus as the Chancellor: Jesus was an influencer and leader, and was also articulate in His communication. When Jesus gave the Beatitudes, He did it at a time people wanted to follow Him for "the blessings" and the "good times". He reminded them of the other side of the coin, and that godliness of character is sometimes refined in less than ideal situations. *Matthew 5*

Graph Characteristics: The Chancellor's graph is D/I/C, characterized by having the "D", the "I" and the "C" traits being exhibited above the midline, while only the "S" trait remains below the midline. The relative position of the "I" and the "S" after the "D" will determine if the individual is more communication focused (higher "I") or more detail focused and legalistic (higher "C").

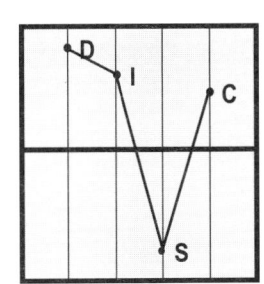

Communicator/Persuader/One Who Promotes

Communicator

Individuals who are **Communicators** exhibit enthusiasm and optimism; they accomplish goals through people. They love being around people, and therefore prefer not to work alone, believing "the more, the merrier." Operating with a high energy level, Communicators may become careless and disorganized. Their communication skills are significantly above average. They desire social recognition and fear the loss of acceptance. When a difficult situation arises, a Communicator is most likely to express every last feeling or withdraw to an emotionally safe position. Communicators trust people very easily and appreciate receiving that trust in return. It is important for Communicators to consciously and truly listen to people around them instead of thinking of what they are about to say next. Inspiring and sometimes flattering, Communicators use their enthusiasm to generate a friendly and team oriented environment.

Communicators in Scripture:	Scripture Verses To Study
Aaron	Exodus 4:14-17, 32:1-6
Andrew	John 1:41
Samaritan Woman	John 4:5-42

Aaron: God gave Aaron his ability to speak so he could assist Moses in his task of communicating to Pharaoh for the release of the Israelite nation being kept as slaves. He thrived when he was around people and at the center of attention, as we find him in Exodus 32. In his desire for acceptance, he succumbed to the people's request for an idol, allowing his fear of rejection to rule his decision. Nevertheless, throughout his entire life Aaron was a passionate leader.

Andrew: Andrew always enjoyed being in the middle of the action. His desire to involve others is first seen in John 1:41. The first thing he did when he heard about Jesus was to run and get his brother Simon, whom Jesus called Peter. True to the Communicator style, Andrew loved being around the crowds and promoting Jesus. Later in his life, he went on to preach the Gospel to many Asiatic nations. His message and his communications skill was so powerful that news of his arrival preceded him to Edessa where he was martyred.

Samaritan Woman: When she first encountered Jesus, this woman's great desire for love and acceptance had placed her in a questionable situation. Open and ready for any communication, she jumped on the opportunity to speak with Jesus despite the social rules prohibiting such interaction. In learning the truth about Christ, her first instinct was to run back to her village and share the good news with all. Her promoting of Jesus' insight to her townspeople brought many to Christ that day.

Jesus as the Communicator: Jesus was a great communicator, the Master of the spoken word. His passionate teaching could captivate great crowds for days at a time. *During those days another large crowd gathered. Since they had nothing to eat, Jesus called his disciples to him and said, "I have compassion for these people; they have already been with me three days and have nothing to eat."* Mark 8:1,2

Graph Characteristics: The Communicator's graph is a pure "I", characterized by having only the "I" trait being exhibited above the midline, while the "D", the "S" and the "C" traits remain below the midline.

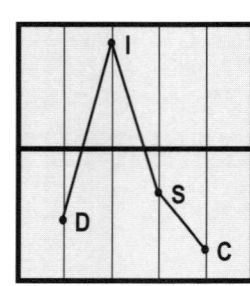

Concluder/Doer/One Who Gets Results

Individuals who are **Concluders** exhibit a tendency to be strong individualists. They are visionary, progressive, and work hard to attain goals. They are forceful and direct. Concluders are curious and have a wide range of interests. At times, they may appear to be cold or blunt because their task-orientation tends to overtake their people-orientation. Concluders place high standards on themselves and those around them, expecting goals to be met. They might appear to be critical when these standards are not met. Because they can have a very strong impact on people and motivate them to achieve their goals, Concluders need to be especially sensitive to others around them. Concluders tend to be short-tempered, especially when they feel that someone is taking advantage of them, for that is one of their greatest fears. Thriving on activity, Concluders are constantly moving forward; they get very frustrated when there is no goal they can strive to achieve.

Concluders in Scripture:	**Scripture Verses To Study**
Joshua	Joshua 1
Noah	Genesis 6-9
Queen of Sheba	1 Kings 10, 2 Chronicles 9
Sarah	Genesis 16, 1 Peter 3:6

Joshua: Joshua's results-oriented characteristics were invaluable to his task as he assumed leadership of Israel. He directed the Israelites through many battles as they took the Promised Land. The action part of Joshua was so strong that the people believed in his leadership. Rarely does he ask anyone to do something, choosing instead to take the role of a commander and lead the people. As a result of his leadership and his ability to deal with conflict, Israel claimed the Promised Land.

Noah: Noah was a progressive doer in his time. Anyone who spends 100 years building a boat when they have never seen rain is progressive and determined. His independent style won him the favor of God in a time when mankind had become corrupt and evil. Noah shone as a light in the darkness, wasting no time in building the ark when God commanded. He directed the construction and collected the animals with little notice of neighbors' opinions. Noah's manifest determination to always do what was right and acceptable in God's eyes brought him to the conclusion of his task.

Queen of Sheba: The queen heard of Solomon's greatness, which translated as perfection in her eyes. She wanted to see if Solomon could meet her standards of perfection; and this drove her to seek him out and immediately test him. She found the communication skills of the Concluder helpful when she communicated that he had passed her test and she desired to keep their foreign relations strong.

Sarah: Sarah exhibited a strong goal-oriented focus in her desire to have children. She commanded her husband to lay with her servant, Hagar in order that she might have children. Her sensitive nature was evident as she became upset when relationships were not pleasing to her, especially with Hagar.

Jesus as the Concluder: Jesus was always visionary, and boldly professed what His Father had sent Him to do. This was exhibited when He stood up in his hometown Temple and read the scriptures, and then proclaimed they were about Him! *"The Spirit of the Lord is on me, because he has anointed me to preach good news to the poor. He has sent me to proclaim freedom for the prisoners and recovery of sight for the blind, to release the oppressed, to proclaim the year of the Lord's favor. Then he rolled up the scroll, gave it back to the attendant and sat down. The eyes of everyone in the synagogue were fastened on him, and he began by saying to them, "Today this scripture is fulfilled in your hearing." Luke 4:18-21*

Graph Characteristics: The Concluder's graph is D/I, characterized by having both the "D" and the "I" traits being exhibited above the midline, while both the "S" and the "C" traits remain below the midline. This is a very active, fast-paced style.

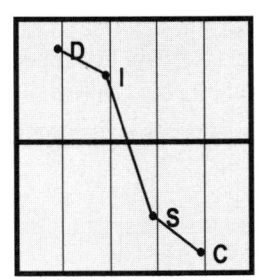

© Copyright 2000-2020 by The Institute for Motivational Living, Inc. All Rights Reserved.

Contemplator/Processor/One Who Ponders

Contemplator

Individuals who are **Contemplators** exhibit a determination for the quality and completion of tasks. Being analytical and logical, they are detail oriented and have high standards for themselves and others. Contemplators are very centered on the task at hand, and are steady and dependable. They are selective and analytical in relationships, thinking processes, and work situations. First evaluating the facts and figures, they will take their time in making decisions, for they want to be precise. However, they also operate with a competitive edge as they seek to accomplish the task. Since a Contemplator's fear is ridicule or criticism, they are sensitive to the people around them and strive to do their best. When a Contemplator is involved, a job will always advance and quality will never be compromised. The personal element in the Contemplator's character gives them a concern and appreciation for relationships. Contemplators are natural peacemakers because they possess the ability to logically analyze a situation ("C"), have a concern for the relationships and a desire to preserve them ("S"), and the decisiveness to bring parties together to deal with one another ("D").

Contemplators in Scripture:
Jeremiah
Zipporah - Wife of Moses

Scripture Verses To Study
Jeremiah 1,9
Exodus 2,4, and 18

Jeremiah: This prophet lived an intense, yet lonely, life. Being extremely task-oriented and obedient to God, he was quick to assume his position once God called him (Jeremiah 1:5). Knowing Jeremiah's fears of ridicule and criticism, He exhorts his servant in Jeremiah 1:17-19. As he obeys God's command, Jeremiah's attention to specifics emerges. His book traces a very detailed, compliant life lived wholly unto God. Jeremiah's goal-oriented nature keeps him centered on his task of standing up for God and speaking His word in spite of rejection and persecution. He was careful to do all God commanded - the right way!

Zipporah: Moses's Midianite wife, Zipporah held to the customs of her homeland. True to the internal standards to which she complied, she did not circumcise her son, Gershom, because it was not in accordance with her beliefs. This demonstrates the Contemplator's tendency toward compliance to rules and regulations, but only ones they respect. She did not welcome change very easily, for she preferred to take her time in making a decision. However, when Moses' life was endangered in Exodus 4: 24, her decisive nature rose as she conceded to God and quickly circumcised her son in order to save Moses' life. She became cold in her reaction to pressure, but ultimately obeyed God.

Jesus as the Contemplator: Jesus exhibited this personality as He dealt with the Samaritan woman at the well. He knew her life story, and was compassionate to the woman but at the same time confronted the sin. By Jesus showing warmth and compassion, the woman regained her self esteem and went into the town boldly professing Christ. *Jesus answered, "Everyone who drinks this water will be thirsty again, but whoever drinks the water I give him will never thirst. Indeed, the water I give him will become in him a spring of water welling up to eternal life." The woman said to him, "Sir, give me this water so that I won't get thirsty and have to keep coming here to draw water." John 4:13-15*

Graph Characteristics: The Contemplator's graph is C/D/S, characterized by having the "C", "D", and "S" traits being exhibited above the midline, while the "I" remains below the midline. The "S" will be the lowest above the midline.

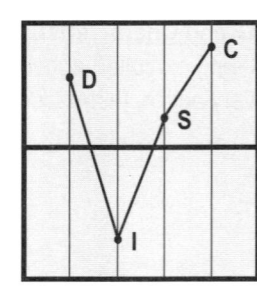

Designer/Administrator/One Who Creates

Individuals who are **Designers** exhibit a high task-orientation and are very sensitive to problems. They are creative, determined, and analytical in their approach to effective problem solving, never accepting a "quick fix." Their goal is to have everything correct and in control while simultaneously avoiding failure. Designers are able to initiate change and improvements, because of their administrative skills. Because they sometimes feel that they are the only ones that can do a job right, Designers will sometimes get bogged down and not allow others to help. Under pressure, they may come across to others as aggressive or stubborn. It is important for Designers to be sensitive to the needs of others around them in order to insure a positive environment. Since Designers value accuracy and precision, high standards are maintained in all aspects of a Designer's work life.

Designers In Scripture:	Scripture Verses To Study
Bezaleel	Exodus 35:30-36:8, 37:1-9
Jochebed	Exodus 1:22-2:4
Jethro	Exodus 2,18

Bezaleel: This man had been handpicked by God to be one of the chief architects of the temple in Moses' time. In Exodus 36, Moses tells the people that he is to not only construct, but teach as well. Bezaleel's high personal standards would require nothing less than absolute perfection in the construction of God's temple. Exodus 37:1-9 recounts the exact steps he took in creating the ark, and he is very precise. His task-orientation would be required in his teaching and overseeing of the entire project. As a Designer, Bezaleel was a man able to meet the high standards required to build the ark and the tabernacle.

Jochebed: Although Moses' mother is silent in this passage, we clearly see her creative problem-solving skills at work to save her son's life. She knew that her task was to save her son and, thanks to her determined nature, save him she did. She was very focused on what to do, not only how she felt. As a mother, she loved her son, and stubbornly worked to save him in spite of Pharaoh's order.

Jethro: As Jethro entered the picture, the first thing he did was ask "Why" questions (as any Designer would do), searching out the facts. He then commanded his daughters to invite Moses to their house, taking charge and determining the best course of action. Jethro worked with the same problem-solving skills when he joins Moses in Exodus 18. Notice that he did not wait for an invitation to visit his son-in-law; he simply informed Moses of his visit plans. After assessing the management situation, Jethro gave Moses detailed instructions as to how he should set up officials, giving detailed reasons to back up the procedure prescribed. This was not a quick fix; it was a Designer setting up a detailed administrative structure and doing things "the right way".

Jesus as the Designer: Jesus was precise in the design of his death and resurrection. The exact plan of redemption was known to Jesus, and it was His will to complete the work to the last detail. *Then the Jews demanded of him, "What miraculous sign can you show us to prove your authority to do all this?" Jesus answered them, "Destroy this temple, and I will raise it again in three days." The Jews replied, "It has taken forty-six years to build this temple, and you are going to raise it in three days?" But the temple he had spoken of was his body. After he was raised from the dead, his disciples recalled what he had said. Then they believed the Scripture and the words that Jesus had spoken* John 2:18-22

Graph Characteristics: The Designer's graph is C/D, characterized by having both the "C" and the "D" traits being exhibited above the midline, while both the "I" and the "S" traits remain below the midline. The "C" will be higher above the midline than the "D".

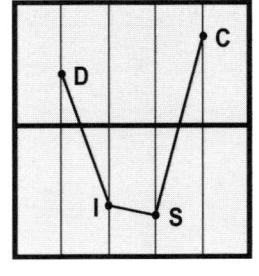

Director/Visionary/One Who Forges Ahead

Director

Individuals who are **Directors** exhibit a fascinating ability to move people and tasks in a forward direction because of their vision and people skills. Energetic and social, they tend to focus on overall goals or the "big picture," and may overlook details. Their focus allows them to be very assertive in rallying others to adopt their vision. In any stressful situation a Director will act with gritty determination and persevere to the end. Conflicts may arise rather frequently, but they do not dissuade Directors. They need freedom to do things the way they believe things should be done and to be able to work at their own pace, which is usually ahead of most others. It is very beneficial for a Director to look to others who possess analytical skills to accumulate needed facts and figures so the details will be attended to. They appreciate loyalty and love to help others reach their goals. Directors are creative, hard working, and driven to achieve winning results.

Directors in Scripture:	**Scripture Verses To Study**
Deborah	Judges 4-5
Samson	Judges 13-16
Ehud	Judges 3

Deborah: This Israeli judge was a woman of great valor. Underneath her palm tree, she imparted the Lord's wisdom to all who sought her. Deborah was very much concerned with those around her, and she spent all day speaking with people. She also cared for the conflicts in their relationships, striving to settle legal cases and keep the peace among the people. Her leadership skills surfaced as she commanded Barak to come to her and receive the word God gave for him. She gave him the general plan for how he must raise an army and defeat the enemy, but specifics how to accomplish that were left in his hands. Deborah literally directed the army towards a victory, for once God gave the word, she persisted until the very end.

Samson: This man of action was quicker to jump than he was to think. As soon as he had a goal in mind, he set out to accomplish it immediately, with or without help. In his early days, Samson's quick decisions and determination made quite a name for him. However, when Delilah persisted in discovering the secret of his strength, his desire to win favor in her eyes overruled the minor detail that he was putting himself in the face of danger. It might be said that people were his greatest weakness, and also his greatest strength. To see his captors worshipping another god and making fun of him drove him to a powerful scene of self-sacrifice for the glory of God.

Ehud: Ehud carried himself in such a way that even kings listened when he gave the command. Like any Director, Ehud possessed significant communication skills. Ehud was so persuasive that he convinced King Eglon to speak with him in private, which put the royalty in a risky situation. His decisiveness was audible in his voice and visible in his determination to rid his people of Eglon's tyranny. With his eyes fixed on his goal, Ehud delivered the "message from God" by means of his sword, killed the king, and rallied the Israelites to a glorious success in battle, returning peace to the land.

Jesus as the Director: Many times Jesus talked about the importance of the "big" picture, and not to be caught up in the details of the law. *When the Pharisees saw this, they asked his disciples, "Why does your teacher eat with tax collectors and 'sinners'?" On hearing this, Jesus said, "It is not the healthy who need a doctor, but the sick. But go and learn what this means: 'I desire mercy, not sacrifice.' For I have not come to call the righteous, but sinners." Matthew 9:11-13*

Graph Characteristics: The Director's graph is D/I/S, characterized by having the "D", the "I" and the "S" traits being exhibited above the midline, while only the "C" trait remains below the midline.

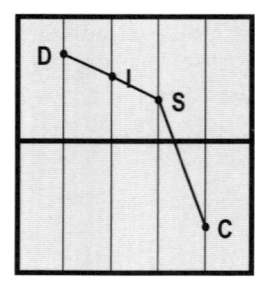

Establisher/Visionary/One Who Develops

Individuals who are **Establishers** exhibit a powerful, individualistic approach, especially towards new challenges and opportunities; they frequently demonstrate a high ego strength. Establishers want excitement and sometimes jump into new adventures before thinking them through fully. They can make demands upon people and situations in order to accomplish their goals, and may be very direct and uncommunicative under pressure. Although they don't always collect facts before making a decision. Establishers like to win at any cost. Establishers are opportunity creators; they possess a vision of the 'big picture' and can move a project forward with great enthusiasm. When they are caught up in accomplishing the task, they may tend to ignore the emotional side of the people involved. Establishers should strive to achieve self-control and self-discipline while cultivating their emotional side in order to be more sensitive of others' feelings and perceived as friendly. Risk takers, people see them as bold, confident, and courageous. Establishers are great visionaries who possess the enthusiasm to make a new idea work without letting obstacles get in the way.

Establishers In Scripture:
Nehemiah
Lydia

Scripture Verses To Study
Nehemiah 2 and 3
Acts 16:13-15, 40

Nehemiah: When faced with a challenge of restoring Jerusalem, Nehemiah focused on his task, and set out to accomplish it as soon as possible. He was so fixated on the task of rebuilding the wall of Jerusalem that it consumed him, even to the point that the king took notice. As soon as the king inquired, Nehemiah immediately shared his plan and used his visionary enthusiasm to convince the king to let him go rebuild Jerusalem's wall. Showing the goal orientation of the Establisher, he was anxious to get the project underway. Also typical of the directive nature of the Establisher's style, Nehemiah oversaw the project by himself while delegating the smaller parts of building the wall to all the citizens. Not even the combined opposition of five enemies was enough to dissuade him from accomplishing his task. He strongly chose to work with a trowel in one hand and a sword in the other.

Lydia: It was especially difficult for women to succeed in the business world of old. However, Lydia rose to the occasion, and with a true determination, she took each new day as it came. She appears to have built her considerable reputation on her achievements. This self-starter also translated her faith into action as she immediately took a strong stand for her God and all the believers. As a successful businesswoman, she combined her drive and determination with a passion for God. Unafraid of public opinion, she invited men to her home (Acts 16:15). She was driven more by her goal (to worship God) than by public impression.

Jesus as the Establisher: Jesus was in charge; and at times He was consumed with a holy passion. Jesus displayed the confrontational elements of this style when he cleared the temple. We see His determination and goal-orientation as He climbs Calvary for us. Remember, Jesus was not a victim on the cross, He was driven to its shame out of His unmitigated love for us. The nails did not hold Him to the cross; it was His commitment to us. *His disciples remembered that it is written: "Zeal for your house will consume me." John 2:17*

Graph Characteristics: The Establisher's graph is a pure "D", characterized by having only the "D" trait being exhibited above the midline, while the "I", the "S" and the "C" traits remain below the midline.

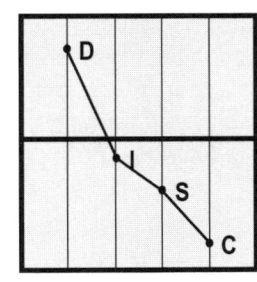

Governor/Pilot/One Who Wins Over

Governor

Individuals who are **Governors** exhibit a high-energy factor, excellent communication skills, and are caring and sensitive in nature. They are direct, friendly, can be enthusiastic, prefer to be informal, and can be somewhat talkative. Since their greatest fears are rejection, criticism, and the loss of security, they may worry too much about what others think. Governors want to be accepted as members of the team and like to know exactly what is expected before they start new projects. They are equipped with the ability to serve as a dominant leader if the parameters of authority are clearly defined, and prefer to lead rather than to follow. They are very conscious about the quality of their work and expect that they will receive social approval for a "job well done." Governors use their excellent communication skills to influence people with their knowledge of facts and their ability to analyze people and situations. They are sincerely concerned about those around them and will work for "win-win" results and resolutions.

Governors In Scripture:	Scripture Verses To Study
David	1 Samuel 16-21
Gideon	Judges 6-7
Naomi	Ruth 1-4

David: True to the Governor pattern, we see great creativity in David; we find that he was a talented musician in 1 Sam 16:18. He was also a strong speaker. He obeyed his superiors and did all that he was commanded while never failing to maintain his social status, as any Governor would do. Using his people skills, David learned of Goliath by discussing current events with some nearby soldiers. This shepherd/warrior successfully calculated the exact strike that would bring Goliath down. David was a man who got things done right - the first time. David was asked to enter Saul's court, and he soon won the favor of all around him. Even as Saul sought to have David killed, his many friends kept him safe and alive. He was very precise, following directions to the letter. As a result of his faithfulness, the Lord placed him as king over Israel.

Gideon: This mighty commander of Israel's army is first seen as hesitant and slow to accept change. His cautious nature was evident as he asks God for definite signs so that he might be reassured, without a doubt in his mind, that he would succeed in overtaking Israel's oppressors. His desire to maintain stability and security was challenged as God called him very far out of his comfort zone into battle **after** removing the majority of his "team". However, once he was sure of his position, Gideon rose to lead the Israelites to an overwhelming victory over Midian with the leadership, communication and encouragement so typical of this style.

Naomi: Naomi was never a woman to hide her feelings. In all that she said and did, her emotions were evident - from her desire to change her name to her excitement in sharing her plan about Boaz with Ruth. Primarily a "people person," Naomi won favor with all. Her desire for stability and roots is seen as she decided to return to Bethlehem, her hometown, where she knew everyone and feet safe there. Her attention to detail and her logic emerge as Naomi instructed Ruth concerning Boaz. This was a woman who truly accomplished the Governor's desire for "win-win" results.

Jesus as the Governor: Jesus was always people oriented and performed many of His miracles out of compassion. Jesus, while always listening to what the Father would have Him do, was comfortable taking charge of any situation because He already knew what His Father had planned for Him. *So they took away the stone. Then Jesus looked up and said, "Father, I thank you that you have heard me. I knew that you always hear me, but I said this for the benefit of the people standing here, that they may believe that you sent me." When he had said this, Jesus called in a loud voice, "Lazarus, come out!" The dead man came out, his hands and feet wrapped with strips of linen, and a cloth around his face. Jesus said to them, "Take off the grave clothes and let him go." John 11:41-44*

Graph Characteristics: The Governor's graph is either I/S/C or I/C/S, characterized by having the "I", the "S" and the "C" traits being exhibited above the midline, while only the "D" trait remains below the midline. The "I" characteristic is in the highest position. The higher the "I", the more animated and communicative the individual will tend to be. In any combination, the I/S/C blend can behave with the decisiveness and determination of a "D" if their parameters are clearly identified.

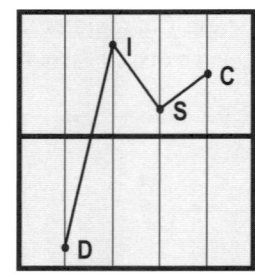

Influencer/Advancer/One Who Inspires

Individuals who are **Influencers** exhibit a high-powered nature coupled with the ability to take a creative idea and make it serve a practical purpose. They are likable people who are motivated both by completing tasks and building relationships. Activity, energy, variety, and change excite them. The equal "D" and "I" combination makes them a very active personality style. Influencers are confident, goal minded, and they convince people to help them because of their outgoing and persuasive manner. They will work on and complete projects independent of any assistance, if necessary, but prefer to work with people. Influencers may be impatient and have little time for details; consequently, interest in a project may be lost once the challenge is gone. They are excellent communicators and have a true interest in people. Since they appreciate people who communicate clearly and concisely, Influencers are not afraid of a good debate. Though they are good leaders and problem solvers; Influencers would do well to pace themselves and take time to relax in their whirlwind life.

Influencers In Scripture:	Scripture Verses To Study
Apollos	Acts 18:24-28
Joseph, son of Jacob	Gen 37, 39-41
Stephen	Acts 6-7

Apollos: Apollos was a man who spoke with great passion and confidence concerning the Lord. In Acts 18:26, the Bible even refers to him as speaking "boldly", displaying drive to accomplish his goal and to communicate his ideas. His passion to tell others about Jesus drove him to strongly assert his beliefs in the synagogue. True to an Influencer style, Apollos fervently debated the Jews in public without hesitation. He was an inspiration to all believers.

Joseph, son of Jacob: Joseph was never afraid to speak his mind, nor was he one to be easily dissuaded from his principles and positions. He confidently told his brothers of his dreams, repeatedly refused Potiphar's wife's invitations, and continually pushed ahead in all situations. Even in prison, Joseph rose to the challenges of position and gained favor in the eyes of all. Always striving to do his best, Joseph utilized his verbal skills by interpreting Pharaoh's dream for him. Joseph's persistence paid off as he was promoted to be second only to Pharaoh.

Stephen: Stephen's strong resolve and powerful message brought him into many confrontational situations. His excellent communication ability enabled him to share the message of Christ with all, while his goal-oriented nature drove him on in his task. Comfortable, confident, and uncompromising, even in a high-risk situation before the Sanhedrin, Stephen boldly confronted all with the truth of Jesus.

Jesus as the Influencer: Jesus exercised influence over crowds and authority over sickness and sin. One minute Jesus would be teaching, and the next He may be taking authority over the works of the enemy. *When Jesus saw their faith, he said to the paralytic, "Son, your sins are forgiven." Now some teachers of the law were sitting there, thinking to themselves, "Why does this fellow talk like that? He's blaspheming! Who can forgive sins but God alone?" Immediately Jesus knew in his spirit that this was what they were thinking in their hearts, and he said to them, "Why are you thinking these things? Which is easier: to say to the paralytic, 'Your sins are forgiven,' or to say, 'Get up, take your mat and walk'? But that you may know that the Son of Man has authority on earth to forgive sins...." He said to the paralytic, "I tell you, get up, take your mat and go home." He got up, took his mat and walked out in full view of them all. This amazed everyone and they praised God, saying, "We have never seen anything like this!" Mark 2:5-12*

Graph Characteristics: The Influencer's graph has an **equal** "D" and "I", characterized by having both the "D" and the "I" traits being exhibited above the midline at the same height, while both the "S" and the "C" traits remain below the midline.

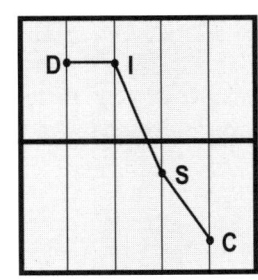

© Copyright 2000-2020 by The Institute for Motivational Living, Inc. All Rights Reserved.

Inquirer/Investigator/One Who Is Consistent

Individuals who are **Inquirers** exhibit a patient, controlled, factual nature combined with a tenacity to accomplish their goals. Considerate, modest individuals, they relate well to most people; however, when necessary, they are able to take a stand. Close relationships are very important to them, but they are selective in choosing their friends. They plan their work carefully, but aggressively, asking questions and collecting data. This is followed by consistent efforts in directed channels. Inquirers with "C" as their secondary characteristic are typically slow to take initiative and do not adapt quickly to change. However, if the "D" is the secondary characteristic, the individual will be more goal-oriented and aggressive in their undertakings. Because of their dogged determination, Inquirers can be successful at many things. They use logic and analysis to make decisions, and they can be firm, almost to the point of stubbornness after making these decisions. Inquirers will rise to challenges and not back down when they have strong feelings about the outcome. They are service oriented and very dependable.

Inquirers In Scripture: **Scripture Verses To Study**
Anna   Luke 2:36-38
Jacob   Genesis 29, 30, 32
James   Acts 15: 13-21

Anna: Anna had waited her whole life for Jesus. In Luke, we see how she demonstrated the stability of her character; she consistently stayed at the temple, never leaving but steadily worshipping, fasting and praying. Her incredible discipline in life is seen as she persistently sought the Lord day and night. Anna's dogged determination allowed her to keep tightly focused on her task of seeking God's redemption.

Jacob: Jacob was a patient, faithful man by the time he came to Laban's family to marry Rachel. He demonstrated his steadfast nature as he agreed to work for seven years in return for the woman he loved. Upon learning of Laban's deception and new proposition, he complied to meet his goal and rose to the challenge of seven more years of labor. Finally, when provoked by Laban's questioning as to why he fled, Jacob was very straightforward and detailed in recapping his last 20 years of service and how he had been wronged. Note that he had all the debts carefully recorded in his mind. Of course, as a detailed individual, he remembered them all. In Genesis 32, as Jacob did not know how Esau would react, his first instinct was to keep the peace. Therefore he divided all his property in half, for safety reasons, and sent gifts to Esau in hopes of appeasing any harsh feelings. He succeeded and God blessed his family.

James: James, although not as outspoken as the apostle Peter, was consistent in his convictions to do things the right way. In Acts 13, James spoke after Peter, Barnabas, and Paul who were all dynamic speakers, and he functioned as a peacemaker, seeking to bring greater understanding on all sides. When he saw the opportunity, his determination and convictions drove him to stand up for what he believed in. He used details and Scripture to thoroughly base the grounds for his opinion. He was not pushy, but he presented a strong case for the Lord.

Jesus as the Inquirer: Jesus often times spent nights of prayer seeking guidance from His Father. Jesus prayed the entire night before selecting His Apostles, and He went to Gethsemene three times to pray the night of His betrayal. *One of those days Jesus went out to a mountainside to pray, and spent the night praying to God. When morning came, he called his disciples to him and chose twelve of them, whom he also designated apostles. Luke 6:12,13*

Graph Characteristics: The Inquirer's graph is either S/D/C or S/C/D, characterized by having the "D", the "S" and the "C" traits being exhibited above the midline, while only the "I" trait remains below the midline. The relative position of the "D" and the "C" will determine if the individual will face inner conflicts over being both expressive and reserved.

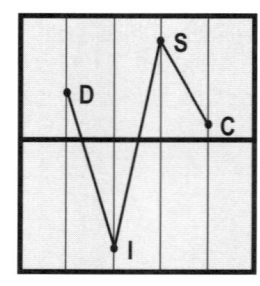

Leader/Decisive/One Who Strengthens

Individuals who are **Leaders** exhibit a high task-orientation while also enjoying people. They will typically be very good at recruiting people for teams or organizations. Leaders are friendly and like to involve others, but they also like to see the tasks done right. Because of their desire to do things correctly, they sometimes appear domineering and aggressive as pressure arises in a situation. It is very beneficial to all when Leaders focus on listening more and considering the needs of others, especially in difficult times. Because of their excellent communication skills, Leaders are able to put strangers at ease and make them comfortable. They influence others using their strong people skills and their ability to reason and be logical; using their verbal skills to encourage and strengthen others. When they are talking and giving opinions and information, they frequently display their ability to establish harmony and unity. Leaders are not bystanders; they are constantly involved. They desire the excitement that comes with new adventures and meeting new people.

Leaders In Scripture:
Ezekiel
Habakkuk
Jude

Scripture Verses To Study
Ezekiel 2,17,37
Habakkuk 1
Jude

Ezekiel: Ezekiel, whose name means "God strengthens," was used by God to prophecy to Israel. The main job of a prophet is to use his verbal skills to communicate a message from God. His prophetic words are vivid and clear. His propensity towards people is clearly seen. However, the force of his character emerges in his determination to continue speaking his message of truth regardless of whether or not people listened. His task orientation is seen especially in his reasoning, his creativity, and his attention to details. Unafraid of danger, Ezekiel spoke out even against his beloved Jerusalem.

Habakkuk: This prophet was a man who wanted answers! Troubled by his observations, he asks difficult questions. His deep concern for the people leads him to seek answers from God. In Habakkuk 1:1 a slightly impatient element emerges, revealing his determination and task-orientation. Also conscientious of details, he has taken note of every word that God said, taking great care to relate the message exactly. Throughout the entire book, Habakkuk expresses his conversation with God in a very descriptive language using the creativity and the verbal skills that characterize this style.

Jude: In his opening paragraphs, Jude revealed his deep concern for people by telling them how he, because of his feelings for them, has decided to change his letter. Originally intending to write to share the good news of salvation, his wanting to include others by encouraging and motivating shows more of his social awareness. His determination to keep believers focused is seen as he relayed what happens to godless men. He used logical reasoning, vivid examples, and details to back up what he said in the letter, all distinctive of the detail-oriented aspect of his character.

Jesus as the Leader: It was a bit ironic, but the boy Jesus was more accepted in the temple than was the grown man. Jesus exhibited at an early age the ability to communicate and to be an influencer of men and women. He taught with authority and clarity never before seen. *After three days they found him in the temple courts, sitting among the teachers, listening to them and asking them questions. Everyone who heard him was amazed at his understanding and his answers. Luke 2:46,47 Because he taught as one who had authority, and not as their teachers of the law. Matthew 7:29*

Graph Characteristics: The Leader's graph is I/D/C, characterized by having the "D", the "I" and the "C" traits being exhibited above the midline, while only the "S" trait remains below the midline. The "I" will be the highest characteristic.

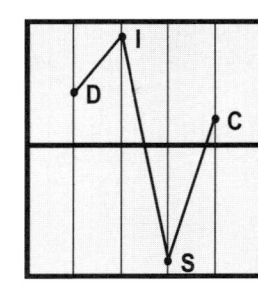

Logical Thinker

Logical Thinker/Analytical/Objective One

Individuals who are **Logical Thinkers** exhibit a practical, proper, and discrete nature. They are self-evaluating and may be critical of both themselves and others, though they seldom voice it, being quiet and reserved. As criticism is their greatest fear, they are constantly striving for perfection. Logical Thinkers internalize information, analyzing issues over and over again. At times they may appear cool and blunt due to their constant analyzing, but by becoming a little more sensitive and adaptable, Logical Thinkers can be seen as more perceptive to the feelings of others. They make decisions slowly based on facts and logic, not emotion, asking "how" and "why" questions. In the eyes of a Logical Thinker, neatness equates with high quality and anything less is unacceptable. They like to plan and organize every area of their life. A stable environment is best for Logical Thinkers as they prefer to be slow and deliberate in their changes, not spontaneous. They require guidelines in their task-oriented work style. Logical Thinkers hold to high standards and constantly strive to meet them.

Logical Thinkers In Scripture:
Luke
Shadrach, Meshach, Abednego
Prophet's Widow

Scripture Verses To Study
Luke 1:1-4, Acts 1:1-2
Daniel 3
2 Kings 4:1-7

Luke: This doctor/author/disciple began his Gospel by telling his audience that he has "carefully investigated everything" and has decided to write an "orderly" account. (Luke 1:3) We see the Logical Thinker's attention to minor elements as Luke traced the events surrounding Jesus' birth, life, death, and resurrection with great detail. No doubt his training as a doctor developed his exactness and precision. Throughout all his writings, Luke used very descriptive language to correctly recount each event and happening. In Acts 1:1-2, Luke was very specific in reviewing what he wrote in his first book, particularly noting that Jesus gave instructions to his disciples. This detail was important to a Logical Thinker, who would properly equate instructions from Jesus as standards to be met.

Shadrach, Meshach, Abednego: These three men lived by the rules of God, and they were willing to die by those rules as well. Exhibiting extremely high personal standards, they chose to abstain from rich foods and eat only vegetables as a means to show proper honor to God. In Daniel 3, the king commands all to worship his idol, but these three young men refused to bow down for they would follow only God's rules and worship only Him. Shadrach, Meshach, and Abednego were consistent with their intrinsic value system and did things the right way - God's way.

Prophet's Widow: Suddenly left without a husband, this widow immediately reacted to her lack of boundaries and safety. Desiring to think things through in a logical manner, she immediately sought the counsel and safety of her husband's leader, Elisha. He asked what she has, and she answers very specifically. After he gave her explicit directions, she was careful to do exactly what she has been instructed to do. When the jars had been collected and filled, she reported back to Elisha for more instructions, seeking to complete her task. This widow obeyed God and was blessed abundantly.

Jesus as the Logical Thinker: Jesus knew scripture, and when the enemy came to Him, Jesus would not allow the enemy to trap Him by twisting scripture. *Jesus said to him, "Away from me, Satan! For it is written: 'Worship the Lord your God, and serve him only.'"*
11 Then the devil left him, and angels came and attended him. Matthew 4:10,11

Graph Characteristics: The Logical Thinker's graph is a pure "C", characterized by having only the "C" trait being exhibited above the midline, while the "D", the "I" and the "S" traits remain below the midline.

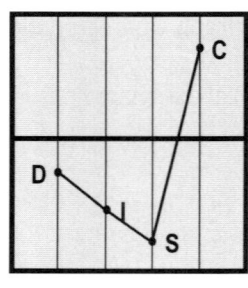

Mediator/Synthesizer/One Who Brings Together

Mediator

Individuals who are **Mediators** exhibit a people-oriented style driven by correctness and loyalty. The main goal of a Mediator is to accomplish a task with a team while maintaining a stable, harmonious environment. Mediators see this as "the right way" to have a relationship. They are friendly, enthusiastic, informal, talkative, and may worry too much about what other people think. Mediators are very sensitive to criticism; therefore, they are very conscious about the quality of their work, especially if they expect to win social approval for a "job well done." They are sensitive to the people around them and will do their best to make the environment pleasing to others. Using their excellent communication skills, Mediators can influence people by their knowledge of facts and ability to analyze people and situations. They do not initiate confrontation, but when confronted have the ability to use their logic to win the case. Mediators will often seek to bring resolution to conflict by exercising their analytical skills (C) and their communication skills (I) to restore and establish relationships (S). They are friendly and flexible, able to adapt very easily.

Mediators In Scripture:	**Scripture Verses To Study**
Midwives (Puah, Shiprah)	Exodus 1:1-21
Matthew	Luke 5:27-32
Silas	Acts 15:22-32, 16:13-40

Midwives: These two women, Puah and Shiprah knew that Pharoh was powerful, but they also knew that God reigned over all. True to the high standards which drove them, they could not and would not go against His law - the order by Pharoh not withstanding. Also demonstrating Mediator characteristics, they persuaded Pharoh with logic concerning the Hebrew mothers' babies. Their people orientation allowed them to be sensitive to the feelings of others – especially the Hebrew mothers bearing children. Wanting to see the families happy and to please God as well, the midwives disobeyed Pharoh and let the male babies live (the "right thing" to do). The loyalty of these midwives came into play when they gave Pharoh an excuse concerning the Hebrews in the attempt to avoid his wrath and keep the peace between all.

Matthew: This tax collector-turned-disciple enjoyed his social time as well as taking care of the details. Matthew's task-over-people nature was a perfect fit for his profession, and more of his attention to tradition and detail is seen in Matthew 1 as he traced the genealogy of Jesus. In Luke 5, however, his social needs surfaced as Matthew held a party where he was able to introduce all of his friends to Jesus, hopefully bringing together a team of believers. He went on to join Jesus' group of 12 disciples, and the stable nature within him held him fiercely loyal to Christ, even to the point of martyrdom. He wrote his gospel from a Jewish perspective, attempting to create a bridge to the Jews by showing how Jesus fulfilled the Law and Prophecies.

Silas: Silas' role in Scripture appears to be a support position. Though there are not many references to him, one evident fact was that Silas' role was that of a team player. His strong respect for legality coupled with his secondary desire to build solid relationships enabled him to effectively remind people of "the rule" with the letter in Acts 15. This is a Mediator desiring to see things done the right way while making sure peace is kept among the brothers. As he traveled with Paul, his loyalty placed him steadily beside Paul at every turn.

Jesus as the Mediator: Jesus was and still is the great Mediator, and He gives us access to the Father and the Holy of Holies; He prays for us as He did His disciples. He was the mediator for the woman caught in adultery, and He mediates for us today. In both cases He looks beyond the sin to the forgiveness He has purchased. *In that day you will ask in my name. I am not saying that I will ask the Father on your behalf. No, the Father himself loves you because you have loved me and have believed that I came from God. I came from the Father and entered the world; now I am leaving the world and going back to the Father." John 16:26-28*

Graph Characteristics: The Mediator's graph is C/I/S, characterized by having the "I", the "S" and the "C" traits being exhibited above the midline, while only the "D" trait remains below the midline. The "C" characteristic is in the highest position. The higher the "C", the more legalistic the individual will tend to be. In any combination, the I/S/C blend can behave with the decisiveness and determination of a "D" if their parameters are clearly identified.

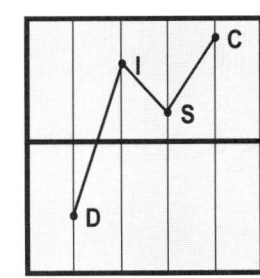

© Copyright 2000-2020 by The Institute for Motivational Living, Inc. All Rights Reserved.

Motivator/Encourager/One Who Is Committed

Motivator

Individuals who are **Motivators** exhibit an encouraging style when motivated by a goal. They prefer to lead or be in charge, but they can also serve as a helper. To be happy and fulfilled in a support role, the Motivator needs recognition and appreciation. Motivators care about the people around them and consider others' feelings in their decision making. Exhibiting excellent abilities to deal with people, they strive to find the way to accomplish tasks quickly and efficiently. Motivators possess strong problem solving skills and prefer to achieve their goals by leading the group through diligence and steadfastness. Determined and enthusiastic, Motivators will eagerly accept challenges and work hard for positive outcomes to situations. They often equate failure and rejection; they need affirmation in these situations. They have the ability to listen creatively and communicate effectively.

Motivators In Scripture: **Scripture Verses To Study**
Titus   Titus 1:5-6:2
Hezekiah   2 Chronicles 32:1-8
Jahaziel   2 Chronicles 20:14-18

Titus: Titus can be viewed as one of Paul's most trusted and able assistants. In Titus 1:5, Paul assigned Titus the task of "troubleshooting". He was given many tasks to accomplish, and his goal-driven nature thrived in this environment. Using his communication skills to demonstrate his strong motivational ability, he was able to effectively assert that authority in which Paul strongly believed. Titus possessed teaching skills, for in Titus 2 Paul instructed him to utilize them in teaching all ages. Titus remained loyal to Paul throughout his whole life. It takes a great motivator to encourage people to live a better life, and Paul recognized that quality in Titus.

Hezekiah: Most of his life, Hezekiah was a faithful king of Judah. In 2 Chronicles 32 he is seen at his best. In light of impending invasion, Hezekiah took the initiative and consulted with his team of officials and military leaders concerning his plan. He knew what he wanted to do and he directed the process of blocking the outside spring, reinforcing the walls and making weapons. Combining his leadership and communication skills, he inspired his people on to victory. Hezekiah remained loyal to his people and his God.

Jahaziel: Jahaziel was a fearless Levite who rallied all the people together, including the king. As the Moabite and Ammonite enemies stormed the borders of Judah, Jahaziel went boldly before the king, and delivered his message. God used Jahaziel to communicate God's promises, thus motivating the people and spurring them on to victory. The desire to see people join together led him to call the entire nation of Judah together to accomplish the task as a united team.

Jesus as the Motivator: Jesus was able, by His words, actions, and example, to motivate others to go out and preach the gospel. He encouraged them and motivated them to action even when they would face difficulties and possible persecution. *After this the Lord appointed seventy-two others and sent them two by two ahead of him to every town and place where he was about to go. He told them, "The harvest is plentiful, but the workers are few. Ask the Lord of the harvest, therefore, to send out workers into his harvest field. Go! I am sending you out like lambs among wolves." Luke 10:1-3*

Graph Characteristics: The Motivator's graph is I/S/D, characterized by having the "D", the "I" and the "S" traits being exhibited above the midline, while only the "C" trait remains below the midline. The "I" characteristic will be the highest on the graph.

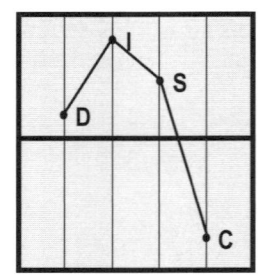

Peacemaker/Diplomat/One Who Is Faithful

Individuals who are **Peacemakers** exhibit a kind nature that is also very detail oriented. They care about people and possess the qualities that make them very meticulous at task completion. They want a steady environment which promotes security. Usually, they like to think issues through carefully, weighing how a decision will affect people. Peacemakers want facts and figures before they will make a decision. They feel uneasy when put in a situation where they feel deserted, or when forced to make a quick decision; especially if their decision will affect others. Peacemakers like people, but prefer to only have a few close friends. Given a choice, they would choose a small group rather than a crowd. Since they are highly sensitive, Peacemakers do not handle criticism well, as they have tried to do their best. Exactness is imperative in everything Peacemakers do. Often keeping their feelings to themselves, others may not be aware of their strong beliefs. Peacemakers are loyal to the leaders they support, and are excellent people to have on the team.

Peacemakers In Scripture:	**Scripture Verses To Study**
Moses	Exodus 3,4,20,32
John	John 19:26-27
Eliezer	Genesis 24

Moses: God took Moses out of his comfort zone and raised him up as His personal representative to lead the Israelites out of Egypt to the Promised Land. Moses was content with the stability of his life as a shepherd. However, when God calls him to go to Pharaoh, Moses immediately becomes fearful, stubbornly questioning God in Exodus 3 and 4 and seeking exact information to specifically direct him should certain situations arise. His detailed nature being somewhat satisfied by the end of the discussion, this allows his loyalty to be displayed as he decides to obey God and complete his assignment. He steadily led the people for decades, following God all the while. We see the Peacemaker speaking to God for the nation of Israel, and speaking to Israel for God.

John: John remained a faithful, devoted disciple of Jesus to his very last day. His loyalty to Jesus brought him to the cross when all of the other disciples fled. Jesus saw him and acknowledged him as a brother, entrusting to him the care of his mother in John 19:26-27. Displaying the determination that characterizes his style, John obeyed Jesus completely and from that day on took Mary into his home, treating her as his own mother. Taking great care to record many emotional details in his writings by focusing on people and feelings, John was faithful to God throughout the rest of his life. His faithfulness as a representative of God is evident in all he did.

Eliezer: Abraham's chosen servant, he was sent as a diplomat to find a suitable wife for Isaac in Genesis 24. His entire life as a servant exemplified loyalty as he remained in a secure environment carefully following all orders from his master. As Abraham sent him to find a wife, Eliezer's detail-oriented nature asks for specifics in completing his mission. In Genesis 24:14, he asked God for a clear and certain proof so that he will be sure of whom he is to choose for Abraham. In a true Diplomat style, Eliezer carefully explained to Rebekah's family every last detail of why he is there, as this is how he would prefer people to communicate with him. Finally, his mission complete, the faithful servant returned to Abraham with Rebekah.

Jesus as the Peacemaker: Jesus would willingly serve and put Himself in the position of the least. However, Jesus used these opportunities to establish important truths in His disciples. He showed them how they were to be compliant to a role of a servant and exhibit brotherly love, and that would gain them to the highest reward in the kingdom. *After that, he poured water into a basin and began to wash his disciples' feet, drying them with the towel that was wrapped around him. He came to Simon Peter, who said to him, "Lord, are you going to wash my feet?" Jesus replied, "You do not realize now what I am doing, but later you will understand." "No," said Peter, "you shall never wash my feet." Jesus answered, "Unless I wash you, you have no part with me." "Then, Lord," Simon Peter replied, "not just my feet but my hands and my head as well!" John 13:5-9*

Graph Characteristics: The Peacemaker's graph is S/C, characterized by having both the "S" and the "C" traits being exhibited above the midline, while both the "D" and the "I" traits remain below the midline. It is the higher "S" characteristic that gives the Peacemaker the team oriented view they possess differentiating them from the C/S – Precisionist.

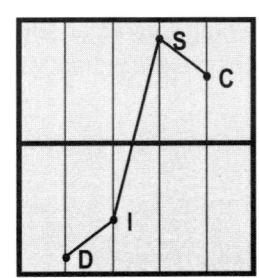

Persuader/Convincer/One Who Influences

Persuader

Individuals who are **Persuaders** exhibit an outgoing spirit, a high interest in people, and the ability to gain respect and admiration from varied types of individuals. They do business in a friendly way, while striving to win others to their objectives and promote their point of view. Persuaders prefer freedom from routine, and they want authority as well as prestige. They need a variety of activities and work more efficiently when others provide analytical data. They thrive when given assignments requiring mobility and challenge. They may come across as nervous or fidgety, because they are always in the middle of some activity. Persuaders would do well to remember that they do not always have to take the lead position, and that they can be a supporter or helper as well. Persuaders want the people around them to communicate efficiently and effectively. Sometimes Persuaders may be viewed by others as overconfident. They may also seem aggressive or pushy; but this is simply a mechanism for avoiding their fears - rejection and being taken advantage of. Overall, they are optimistic and motivating. Persuaders know how to get results through people!

Persuaders In Scripture:	**Scripture Verses To Study**
John the Baptist	Luke 3
Peter	Matthew 16 and 26, Acts 3
Rebekah	Genesis 24

<u>John the Baptist:</u> John's main purpose in life was to communicate God's message as a true "light in the darkness." His great communication skills caused him to be surrounded by crowds (Luke 3:7 NIV), all of whom were drawn to hear his stirring messages. All day every day, John would call people back to Lord and baptize them as he eagerly awaited the Messiah. John's determined nature emerges in his steely resolve and unrelenting diligence to boldly proclaim sin as sin; he did not hesitate in rebuking anyone for their sins and calling upon them to "repent and prepare the way of the Lord", even if they happened to be king of the realm.

<u>Peter:</u> Peter, the spontaneous and passionate disciple, "shot from the hip" in most situations. He was always the first to speak, even when it may have been wiser to hold his tongue. Peter speaks more than anyone in the New Testament except Jesus. Sometimes, however, in his aggressiveness, he did not stop to think before he spoke; and in Matthew 26 Peter's emotionalism and fear get the best of him and he denied Jesus. Jesus redeemed and restored him. In Acts 3, Peter utilized that same determined nature and his intrinsic communication skills at the temple gate, directing people to repent and turn to God. Peter's great redemptive quality was that his desire to be close to Jesus far outweighed his fear of the unknown. It is perhaps best exemplified as Peter got out of the boat to walk with Jesus in the storm (Matthew 14:29).

<u>Rebekah:</u> Rebekah was a friendly and confident woman. She demonstrated her love for people in being friendly to Abraham's servant, watering his camel, and opening her house to him. The decisive aspect of her character also emerged as she did not hesitate in making the decision to invite the servant to stay for the night. Upon hearing of his mission, she was immediately ready to leave and become Isaac's wife. She was a woman who embraced change and all that God had for her.

<u>Jesus as the Persuader:</u> Jesus was the master communicator, and He was able to take a conversation in the direction He wanted it to go. Jesus was never outmaneuvered in His dealings with the Pharisees. *Jesus replied, "I will also ask you one question. If you answer me, I will tell you by what authority I am doing these things. John's baptism - where did it come from? Was it from heaven, or from men?" They discussed it among themselves and said, "If we say, 'From heaven,' he will ask, 'Then why didn't you believe him?' But if we say, 'From men' - we are afraid of the people, for they all hold that John was a prophet." So they answered Jesus, "We don't know." Then he said, "Neither will I tell you by what authority I am doing these things. Matthew 21:24-27*

<u>Graph Characteristics:</u> The Persuader's graph is I/D, characterized by having both the "I" and the "D" traits being exhibited above the midline, while both the "S" and the "C" traits remain below the midline.

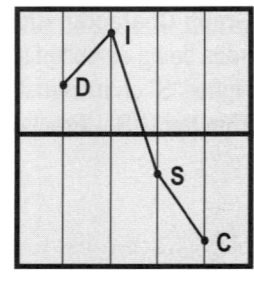

Practitioner/Realist/One Who Is Steadfast

Individuals who are **Practitioners** exhibit an outgoing style with an analytical, cautious disposition. They develop friends easily and control themselves to the extent that they rarely antagonize intentionally. Practitioners are caring, friendly, and competent. Being perfectionistic in nature, they will isolate themselves if necessary to get the job done. Practitioners like to be in predictable situations - "No surprises, please." They are quality oriented individuals who seek approval for a job well done. Practitioners can be counted on to do a good job and pay attention to detail while being aware of the needs of the people around them. They have excellent interaction skills and use their knowledge of facts to influence people. Because they want to be well liked, Practitioners may have a hard time in a disciplinary role. They can be very effective by combining intuitive, logical, and analytical skills with strong people skills. When they develop their skills to their full potential, Practitioners can be very powerful leaders.

Practitioners in Scripture:	Scripture Verses To Study
Elijah	1 Kings 18 and 19
Jonah	Jonah 1-4
Priscilla & Aquilla	Acts 18; I Corinthians 16:19

Elijah: In all that he did, Elijah was careful to properly follow everything that God said, to the letter. His conformity is seen in I Kings 19:2 as he was compliant in doing just what God directed and meeting Ahab. Elijah also exhibited strong communication skills. Typically, Practitioners avoid conflict, however in the case of 1 Kings 18 where he challenged the Baal prophets to have their "god" set a sacrifice on fire, Elijah became critical of their "god's" performance. This demonstrated the fact that the Practitioner will only be pushed "so far" - then they will draw a line and refuse to move. Stubbornly loyal to God, he proved to all at hand that his God is alive and real.

Jonah: Jonah valued his safety and his security. When God calls upon him to go to Nineveh, Jonah, fearing rejection, criticism, and any other potential surprises, ran the other way. In his estimation, He did not feel the Ninevites deserved to be saved, for they were a wicked people who did not meet his standards. In his desire to hold to high standards, Jonah did not think that another chance was warranted. His tendency to fear what he could not control, calculate, or determine overruled his desire to obey God. However, once God convinced him of the plan (with the aid of a large fish), Jonah's compliant character carried him to Nineveh to obey God's instructions. Utilizing his communication skills, Jonah proclaimed such a powerful judgement that the entire city repented and turned to God. When God had mercy on the city and does not destroy them, Jonah's high standards and loyalty to his people were seen once again. God appeared to his concern for people by showing Jonah 120,000 children (those who did not know their right from their left) in the city. God, understanding Jonah perfectly, explained to him through the example of the vine, the reason why God did what He did, appeasing his need for justice.

Priscilla and Aquilla: This couple is always mentioned together in the Bible. Tentmakers by trade, they exhibit high attention to detail by being precise and exact in their profession. Their desire for accuracy motivated them in Acts 18: 26 (NIV), to invite Apollos to their house and "explain the way of the Lord to him more adequately." However, this attention to detail is coupled with a strong concern for the feelings and needs of people. In I Corinthians 16:19, Priscilla and Aquilla allowed their home to be one of the first house churches. Their loving and caring character was seen in a propensity towards people, and they were loyal and steady in their devotion.

Jesus as the Practitioner: Jesus grew up learning a trade to provide for His family. He was the oldest son, and would have provided for them after the apparent death of Joseph in his teen years. He grew in favor with men and God. *Then he went down to Nazareth with them and was obedient to them. But his mother treasured all these things in her heart. And Jesus grew in wisdom and stature, and in favor with God and men.* Luke 2:51, 52

Graph Characteristics: The Practitioner's graph is C/S/I, characterized by having the "I", the "S" and the "C" traits being exhibited above the midline, while only the "D" trait remains below the midline. The "C" characteristic is in the highest position. The higher the "C", the more legalistic the individual will tend to be. In any combination, the I/S/C blend can behave with the decisiveness and determination of a "D" if their parameters are clearly identified.

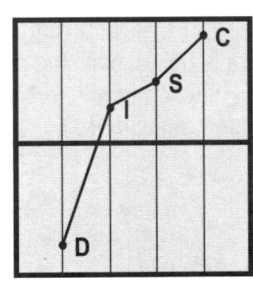

© Copyright 2000-2020 by The Institute for Motivational Living, Inc. All Rights Reserved.

Precisionist/Perfectionist/Traditional One

Precisionist

Individuals who are **Precisionists** exhibit a precise, detailed, stable nature. They are systematic thinkers who tend to follow procedures in both personal and business life. They act in a highly tactful, diplomatic fashion and rarely antagonize their associates consciously, taking care to avoid conflict. Extremely conscientious, they painstakingly require accuracy in work and maintain high standards. Precisionists like a protected and secure environment with set rules and regulations, and dislike sudden changes. They like people, but prefer having only a few close friends. Exactness is of the essence to Precisionists, and criticism (their greatest fear) is equated with failure. They can be counted on to carry out tasks correctly. They want exact facts and figures before they will make a decision, and feel uneasy when forced to decide anything quickly. Predictability and security are the greatest goals for a Precisionist. This is true in all aspects of a Precisionist's life; the more stable the environment, the happier they are.

Precisionists In Scripture:	**Scripture Verses To Study**
Esther	Esther 4
Zechariah	Luke 1
Joseph, Jesus' father	Matthew 1:1-23

Esther: In all that she undertook, Esther cautiously paced herself. As she attempted to comfort her uncle, Mordecai, her love of people was displayed in her concern for others. However, the cautious and precise aspect of her nature took its primary position as she responded to Mordecai explaining why she could not go to the king. In detail, she explained to him the rules of castle life and how she did not wish to jeopardize her security by going to the king without being summoned, risking everything. That same aspect of her nature allowed her to plan exactly how she would obtain the king's favor, obtain her request, and broach the subject of the Jews to the king. It should be noted that she left plenty of time between each stage of the strategy. By careful planning and compassion for her people, Esther saved the day - and God's people.

Zechariah: Father of John the Baptist, Zechariah was a man faithful to tradition. His priestly office required him to know and follow every last law and custom. He found comfort in the routine of service, and the clarity of the expectations. Every day he followed a set routine as a stable and loyal individual. Then God sent him a message that he and his wife would have a child, instructing Zechariah as to his upbringing. This sudden change brought some amount of internal confusion. Unsure of the exact details of how he and his wife would be able to do this, he questioned God's messenger, and asked for proof. In return, God gave him nine months of silence to consider the divine message in detail. By the end of the term, Zechariah understood, believed, and carefully followed God's will.

Joseph: Jesus' father was a quiet man who followed the traditions of his people. His orderly and detailed nature governed everything he did from carpentry, which is an exacting profession, to dealing with people, where he follows the rules. Upon learning of Mary's pregnancy, he could not tolerate her sin (breaking rules) or her betrayal, nor bring criticism upon himself. Therefore, he sought to divorce her quietly. His sensitive and compassionate side emerged in that he did not wish to expose her to public disgrace. But God intervened and answered Joseph's questions. Submissive to the ultimate rule-determiner, Joseph exemplified a man of solid faith and devotion.

Jesus as the Precisionist: Jesus was steady and unmoved by crowd reaction. He knew what had to take place and what had to be done. He was not swayed by popular opinion, but was steady and compliant to His Father's will. *Now while he was in Jerusalem at the Passover Feast, many people saw the miraculous signs he was doing and believed in his name. But Jesus would not entrust himself to them, for he knew all men. He did not need man's testimony about man, for he knew what was in a man. John 2:23-25*

Graph Characteristics: The Precisionist's graph is C/S, characterized by having both the "C" and the "S" traits being exhibited above the midline, while both the "D" and the "I" traits remain below the midline. It is the higher "C" characteristic that gives the Precisionist the detail and/or procedure oriented view they possess differentiating them from the S/C – Diplomat.

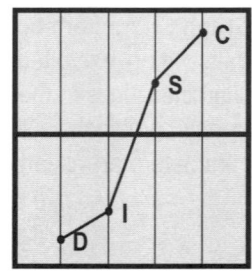

Reformer/Statesman/One Who Commands Respect

Individuals who are **Reformers** exhibit a sociable and friendly nature, but they also like to drive situations and be leaders. They accomplish tasks through their social skills. They are caring and accepting of others. Reformers concentrate on the task at hand until it is completed, but know their limitations and will ask for assistance when necessary. They are able to function not only as team leaders, but team players; and they are happy to share credit with the team. They desire popularity and recognition, and tend to have high trust in others. Reformers are constantly involved with projects and people, and work in the forefront. They use their directness to solve conflicts. They are sensitive to others' feelings and will attempt to create a favorable environment for everyone. They have excellent social skills and possess sincere empathy for people. This makes them good motivators of people. They are optimistic and positive; Reformers always choose the "bright side" when evaluating people or circumstances.

Reformers in Scripture:	Scripture Verses To Study
Isaiah	Isaiah 16, 49
Samuel	1 Samuel 16:1-13
Cornelius	Acts 10

Isaiah: Isaiah is considered to be one of the greatest of the Old Testament prophets. In Isaiah 16, especially verse 9, the expressive aspect of the Reformer in Isaiah emerged as he boldly poured out his feelings. However, his task-orientation and determination allowed him to rebuke all those not walking in obedience with God. Isaiah's caring side arose as he went on to comfort the Israelites throughout the rest of the book. In Chapter 49, Isaiah spoke as a true Reformer, entreating all to hear and rejoice in the Lord. He was a man with passion, conviction, and a message from God.

Samuel: This priest, respected by the entire nation, exemplified the Reformer/Statesman. He acted as God's official in a day when many others had become corrupt. His entire life was a ministry to others on behalf of God, he was truly a people-oriented figure. In I Samuel 16, God directed him to anoint a new king. Displaying the task-oriented aspect of his character, Samuel got right down to business, asking direct questions and seeking to accomplish what he was sent to do. His steady and stable nature held Samuel loyal to God throughout his entire life. This Reformer/Statesman utilized his skills and abilities for the glory of God.

Cornelius: Cornelius, the Roman centurion, sought to accomplish his goals through his social skills. Being a centurion, it was necessary to have strong discipline and communication skills in order to maintain effective control over his troops. Yet his ability to relate well also gave Cornelius influence with those around him, and he "called together his relatives and close friends" (Acts 10:24 NIV) so that they might all meet Peter. Cornelius was a family man, valuing loved ones, stability, and loyalty. This man paved the way as he and his household were the first Gentiles to experience baptism in the Holy Spirit. This proved to be a significant turning point as the eyes of Peter and the other apostles were opened to the fact that even Gentiles were to receive the same outpouring of God's abundance as the Jewish converts.

Jesus as the Reformer: When Jesus first taught the crowd of 5,000 men, and then led His disciples to be part of a great miracle, Jesus was interested in the crowd and the growth of his disciples, and took charge to make sure everything was taken care of. *When Jesus landed and saw a large crowd, he had compassion on them and healed their sick. As evening approached, the disciples came to him and said, "This is a remote place, and it's already getting late. Send the crowds away, so they can go to the villages and buy themselves some food." Jesus replied, "They do not need to go away. You give them something to eat." Matthew 14:14-16*

Graph Characteristics: The Reformer's graph is I/D/S, characterized by having the "D", the "I" and the "S" traits being exhibited above the midline, while only the "S" trait remains below the midline. The "I" characteristic will be the highest on the graph.

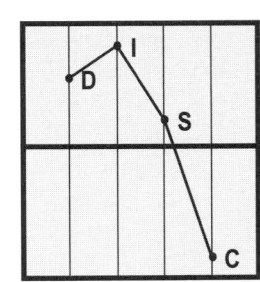

Technician/Specialist/One Who Is Steady

Technician

Individuals who are **Technicians** exhibit a stable, consistent nature by working to maintain an unchanging environment focused around people. Preferring supportive roles, they work well with many of the other personality styles because of their controlled and modest behavior. They are patient, loyal, and helpful to friends. Friendships are developed slowly and selectively. Technicians are not bored by routine and work best with guidelines and rules that are clearly spelled out. Technicians' greatest fear is loss of security, and sudden changes are difficult for them. They need time to adjust to changes and are reluctant to let go of the "old way of doing things." They prefer to approach change as a step-by-step process, not an event. Once a Technician has made a decision, they will tend to stick to it, even stubbornly, because much time has gone into the decision-making process. They have a hard time saying "no," and they seek peace at almost any cost. Avoiding conflict, they tend to internalize their feelings. A Technician will adopt a tenacious attitude, even in tough times; and can be relied upon to stay true through it all. But beware of mistaking their desire for peace as weakness; once you have pushed them to their limit - they are immovable.

Technicians in Scripture:	Scripture Verses To Study
Mary, the mother of Jesus	Luke 1:26-56; John 2
Simeon	Luke 2
Dorcas	Acts 9:36-42

Mary, mother of Jesus: In all that she does, Mary is seen as the loyal, loving mother of Jesus. When the angel informed her that she will bear God's son, her fears were answered by a detailed explanation that included the process, as well as how important a task it would be. Devoted completely to her God, Mary agreed. True to her high desire for peace, Mary was never seen in conflict. In John 2, at the wedding in Cana, Mary avoided confrontation with Jesus by taking an indirect approach, telling the servants to "Do whatever he tells you." She was a supportive mother, valuing her family and friends. Even as Jesus hung on a cross, her incredible loyalty and tenacity were displayed as she stayed at His feet and ignored her own safety.

Simeon: This man had faithfully waited his entire life for "the consolation of Israel" (Luke 2:25). His patience and determination have kept him at the temple awaiting the promised Messiah. There were no changes at the temple; its particular routine was repeated every day, week after week and year after year. Simeon found great security and personal contentment simply waiting for God to fulfill His promise to a devoted servant.

Dorcas: Dorcas did not utter one word in the Bible, but she was extolled for her "supportive" roles to all around her. Acts 9:36 records how she was always doing good and helping the poor. The "always" demonstrates her stability and the reference to her service expresses the aspect of her character as a consistent provider and support to many. She was helpful and dedicated to all around her, but most of all, to her Lord.

Jesus as the Technician: Jesus was a friend, a good shepherd to all who came to Him. He loved children, He loved the unlovable, and was not afraid to touch the untouchable. He is the picture of loyalty. *When Jesus saw this, he was indignant. He said to them, "Let the little children come to me, and do not hinder them, for the kingdom of God belongs to such as these. Mark 10:14*

Graph Characteristics: The Technician's graph is a pure "S", characterized by having only the "S" trait being exhibited above the midline, while the "D", the "I" and the "C" traits remain below the midline.

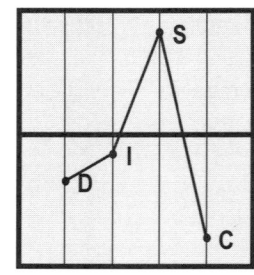